The FBI

CRIME, JUSTICE, AND PUNISHMENT

The FBI

Daniel E. Harmon

Austin Sarat, GENERAL EDITOR

CHELSEA HOUSE PUBLISHERS
Philadelphia

Frontispiece: An FBI team prepares for an armed show-down. Although it is scenes like this one that capture the public imagination, agents of the Federal Bureau of Investigation are more than just brave, well-armed crime fighters. FBI agents are trained in such areas as the law, accounting, forensic science, and psychology.

Chelsea House Publishers

Editor in Chief Sally Cheney
Production Manager Pamela Loos
Art Director Sara Davis
Director of Photography Judy L. Hasday
Managing Editor James D. Gallagher
Senior Production Editor J. Christopher Higgins

Staff for THE FBI

Associate Art Director Takeshi Takahashi
Designer Keith Trego
Picture Researcher Patricia Burns
Cover Designer Keith Trego

First Printing

1 3 5 7 9 8 6 4 2

The Chelsea House World Wide Web address is
http://www.chelseahouse.com

Library of Congress Cataloging-in-Publication Data

Harmon, Daniel E.
The FBI / Daniel E. Harmon.
    p.   cm.   — (Crime, justice, and punishment)
Includes bibliographical references and index.

ISBN 0-7910-4289-8 (alk. paper)

1. United States. Federal Bureau of Investigation—Juvenile
literature. [1. United States. Federal Bureau of Investigation.]
I. Title II. Series.
HV8144.F43 H37 2001
363.25'0973—dc21   00-045155

Contents

CRIME, JUSTICE, AND PUNISHMENT

Fears and Fascinations:

An Introduction to
Crime, Justice, and Punishment

By Austin Sarat

We live with crime and images of crime all around us. Crime evokes in most of us a deep aversion, a feeling of profound vulnerability, but it also evokes an equally deep fascination. Today, in major American cities the fear of crime is a major fact of life, some would say a disproportionate response to the realities of crime. Yet the fear of crime is real, palpable in the quickened steps and furtive glances of people walking down darkened streets. At the same time, we eagerly follow crime stories on television and in movies. We watch with a "who done it" curiosity, eager to see the illicit deed done, the investigation undertaken, the miscreant brought to justice and given his just deserts. On the streets the presence of crime is a reminder of our own vulnerability and the precariousness of our taken-for-granted rights and freedoms. On television and in the movies the crime story gives us a chance to probe our own darker motives, to ask "Is there a criminal within?" as well as to feel the collective satisfaction of seeing justice done.

Fear and fascination, these two poles of our engagement with crime, are, of course, only part of the story. Crime is, after all, a major social and legal problem, not just an issue of our individual psychology. Politicians today use our fear of, and fascination with, crime for political advantage. How we respond to crime, as well as to the political uses of the crime issue, tells us a lot about who we are as a people as well as what we value and what we tolerate. Is our response compassionate or severe? Do we seek to understand or to punish, to enact an angry vengeance or to rehabilitate and welcome the criminal back into our midst? The CRIME, JUSTICE, AND PUNISHMENT series is designed to explore these themes, to ask why we are fearful and fascinated, to probe the meanings and motivations of crimes and criminals and of our responses to them, and, finally, to ask what we can learn about ourselves and the society in which we live by examining our responses to crime.

Crime is always a challenge to the prevailing normative order and a test of the values and commitments of law-abiding people. It is sometimes a Raskolnikov-like act of defiance, an assertion of the unwillingness of some to live according to the rules of conduct laid out by organized society. In this sense, crime marks the limits of the law and reminds us of law's all-too-regular failures. Yet sometimes there is more desperation than defiance in criminal acts; sometimes they signal a deep pathology or need in the criminal. To confront crime is thus also to come face-to-face with the reality of social difference, of class privilege and extreme deprivation, of race and racism, of children neglected, abandoned, or abused whose response is to enact on others what they have experienced themselves. And occasionally crime, or what is labeled a criminal act, represents a call for justice, an appeal to a higher moral order against the inadequacies of existing law.

Figuring out the meaning of crime and the motivations of criminals and whether crime arises from defiance, desperation, or the appeal for justice is never an easy task. The motivations and meanings of crime are as varied as are the persons who engage in criminal conduct. They are as mysterious as any of the mysteries of the human soul. Yet the desire to know the secrets of crime and the criminal is a strong one, for in that knowledge may lie one step on the road to protection, if not an assurance of one's own personal safety. Nonetheless, as strong as that desire may be, there is no available technology that can allow us to know the whys of crime with much confidence, let alone a scientific certainty. We can, however, capture something about crime by studying the defiance, desperation, and quest for justice that may be associated with it. Books in the CRIME, JUSTICE, AND PUNISHMENT series will take up that challenge. They tell stories of crime and criminals, some famous, most not, some glamorous and exciting, most mundane and commonplace.

This series will, in addition, take a sober look at American criminal justice, at the procedures through which we investigate crimes and identify criminals, at the institutions in which innocence or guilt is determined. In these procedures and institutions we confront the thrill of the chase as well as the challenge of protecting the rights of those who defy our laws. It is through the efficiency and dedication of law enforcement that we might capture the criminal; it is in the rare instances of their corruption or brutality that we feel perhaps our deepest betrayal. Police, prosecutors, defense lawyers, judges, and jurors administer criminal justice and in their daily actions give substance to the guarantees of the Bill of Rights. What is an adversarial system of justice? How does it work? Why do we have it? Books in the CRIME, JUSTICE, AND PUNISHMENT series will examine the thrill of the chase as we seek to capture the criminal. They will also reveal the drama and majesty of the criminal trial as well as the day-to-day reality of a criminal justice system in which trials are the exception and negotiated pleas of guilty are the rule.

When the trial is over or the plea has been entered, when we have separated the innocent from the guilty, the moment of punishment has arrived. The injunction to punish the guilty, to respond to pain inflicted by inflicting pain, is as old as civilization itself. "An eye for an eye and a tooth for a tooth" is a biblical reminder that punishment must measure pain for pain. But our response to the criminal must be better than and different from the crime itself. The biblical admonition, along with the constitutional prohibition of "cruel and unusual punishment," signals that we seek to punish justly and to be just not only in the determination of who can and should be punished, but in how we punish as well. But neither reminder tells us what to do with the wrongdoer. Do we rape the rapist, or burn the home of the arsonist? Surely justice and decency say no. But, if not, then how can and should we punish? In a world in which punishment is neither identical to the crime nor an automatic response to it, choices must be made and we must make them. Books in the CRIME, JUSTICE, AND PUNISHMENT series will examine those choices and the practices, and politics, of punishment. How do we punish and why do we punish as we do? What can we learn about the rationality and appropriateness of today's responses to crime by examining our past and its responses? What works? Is there, and can there be, a just measure of pain?

CRIME, JUSTICE, AND PUNISHMENT brings together books on some of the great themes of human social life. The books in this series capture our fear and fascination with crime and examine our responses to it. They remind us of the deadly seriousness of these subjects. They bring together themes in law, literature, and popular culture to challenge us to think again, to think anew, about subjects that go to the heart of who we are and how we can and will live together.

*   *   *   *   *

Among all of the law enforcement agencies in the United States, none is as storied and controversial as the FBI. From the early part of the twentieth century to the present, the FBI has been for some a model of efficient and effective law enforcement. For others it has all too often been an unwelcome tool of repression in a democratic society. Yet whatever one's view, the FBI has occupied a distinctive and important place in the public imagination.

The FBI presents several case histories, stories that will engage the reader and that make the manuscript come alive. It focuses on the FBI as an institution as well as on some of its most controversial tactics. It shows how the FBI's Most Wanted List has blurred the boundary between professional law enforcement and the public and that the use of television dramatically increases the ability of the FBI to expand its network of surveillance. Throughout, it provides a fascinating look at how the FBI balances our desire to catch the bad guys with respect for our rights. Finally, it highlights the way the internationalization of crime poses new and distinctive challenges for the twenty-first century FBI.

FIGHTING
FEDERAL CRIMES

During the morning of April 19, 1995, Americans across the country were silenced and stunned as TV newsbreaks showed a modern office building with one side blown away. Earthquake? No—explosion . . . an explosion of a magnitude not seen in cities outside war zones.

Bomb or accident? The former seemed likely. Although the Alfred P. Murrah Federal Building in Oklahoma City, Oklahoma, was not a national landmark, it was the site of government offices. Was this an isolated act of terrorism? First in a sequence of atrocities? Or the beginning of a terrorist war?

In the coming days, as rescue workers carefully removed bodies and survivors from the rubble of the building, the casualty numbers rose. The final death toll was 168, including children in the building's day care facility for parent-employees. In lives lost, it was the most costly terrorist act ever committed on American soil. Airline bombings, by comparison, have

In 1995 an explosion from a deadly bomb ripped through the Alfred P. Murrah Federal Building in Oklahoma City. The blast took the lives of 168 victims, including children. FBI teams devoted two years to apprehending and prosecuting Timothy McVeigh, the architect of the bombing.

cost hundreds of lives at once. But here was a different kind of danger. If terrorists would target a seemingly ordinary office building in a typical middle-American city . . . they might strike anywhere, anytime, for reasons unforeseen.

Sorting out a massive crime of this nature is a task that involves many law enforcement officials from different agencies, local and federal. In Oklahoma City, work was immediately begun by the organization whose name is synonymous with crime fighting in America: the Federal Bureau of Investigation.

In a sense, conducting a criminal investigation can be like solving a jigsaw puzzle. Some parts come together quickly. Then hours, days, weeks, and perhaps months of tedium follow. Countless numbers of look-alike pieces have to be scrutinized and fit into place until a picture begins to emerge.

As investigators began tracking the bombers, the first major piece of the horrible puzzle was placed on the table: the remains of a rental truck that had been parked just outside the building. Experts identified it as the vehicle that had contained the explosive device.

A careful study of its charred, mangled scraps began immediately. On an axle, agents could make out the vehicle identification number. The second piece of the puzzle was in place.

Here was a solid trail to follow. Officials quickly traced the vehicle ID to a rental office in Junction City, Kansas, 250 miles to the north. Part three of the puzzle was in their grasp. Predictably, they learned that the person who had rented the truck apparently used an alias. But rather than a dead end, the lead ultimately yielded the identification of a prime suspect.

The break resulted from old-fashioned legwork. From employees at the rental office in Junction City, agents learned that two men had rented the suspect truck—two more pieces to the puzzle. Compiling descriptive details, an artist sketched their faces. FBI officers took copies of the drawings door to door in Junction City. They realized that most of the citizens they interviewed would not remember the men even if they had caught a glimpse of them. But they also knew one of the faces may have stuck in the subconscious of some unknowing but important witness.

Their witness turned out to be the owner of a local motel. When shown the sketches, she recognized one of the men as a lodger who had registered on April 12, one week before the bombing. Amazingly, as it turned out, the man had checked in under his real name: Timothy McVeigh.

Even more startling, when they conducted a nationwide computer search to determine whether one "Timothy McVeigh" had an arrest record, they found him close by—in jail! Within two hours of the bombing, McVeigh had been arrested by a traffic patrolman for driving a vehicle with no license tag and, subsequently, charged with carrying a concealed weapon and driving with no auto insurance. He was in jail in the town of Perry, not far from Oklahoma City. Chillingly, by the time FBI agents discovered their suspect there, he was about to get out on bail!

If McVeigh had been released from custody on the traffic and gun possession charges, would he have disappeared? Would the bombing investigation have been thrown into slow gear? It seems probable. On the other hand, McVeigh didn't know at the time that he'd already been identified in connection with the Oklahoma City bombing. Perhaps he believed that by renting the truck under an assumed name in a distant city, he and his accomplice had taken enough precautions to sever any traceable connection between themselves and the crime site. Besides, the truck was bound to be destroyed in the blast. McVeigh had been confident enough in the plan to sign his real name at the Kansas motel. Now, as far as he knew, he was in jail but safe from implication in the bombing, facing only minor,

In a street strewn with rubble from the Murrah building, an FBI agent inspects part of the transmission from the truck that had carried the bomb. Evidence collected by the FBI and other law enforcement agencies formed the backbone of the case against Timothy McVeigh and his conspirators.

unrelated charges.

He didn't count on the skill and doggedness of modern crime fighters.

The pieces of this crime puzzle seemed to be coming together rapidly. Agents had the primary suspect in custody within days of the crime. The puzzle's picture had taken dramatic shape. But to complete it, thousands of agents had to work long, tedious months following up on secondary leads, filling in thousands of details make an ironclad case for the prosecution. In this painstaking process, the FBI was assisted by both the Bureau of Alcohol, Tobacco and Firearms (ATF) and (because a federal building had been targeted) the Secret Service.

Agents learned that McVeigh and a former army buddy, Terry Nichols, had bought (and stolen) large quantities of explosives the previous autumn. These materials included dynamite and ammonium nitrate fertilizer, a highly volatile substance. It's estimated that McVeigh's bomb in Oklahoma City consisted of two tons of explosives. Authorities believe McVeigh and Nichols poured the fertilizer into barrels and mixed it with liquid fuel.

In the days before the bombing, McVeigh bought a used car as his getaway vehicle and rented the truck under a false name. Had it not been for the license plate apparently falling off his car, resulting in the traffic arrest, he might be at large today!

When the puzzle was complete and the case went to trial in 1997, the FBI's star witness was Michael Fortier. In testimony before the jury, he pointed out on a model of the building how the bombing had been planned and carried out. Fortier had helped "case" the building before the bombing.

Fortier, like Nichols, was an old army pal of McVeigh's. McVeigh had been best man at Fortier's wedding. Fortier said McVeigh hated the federal government. McVeigh chose the Murrah Building in Oklahoma City as his bombing target, Fortier testified, after convincing himself that it was there that FBI and ATF officials had planned and coordinated a siege against an extremist group in Texas. The standoff at the Branch Davidian compound near Waco—exactly two years before the Oklahoma City bombing—had ended in fiery death for 80 members of the heavily armed cult.

Although he had assisted McVeigh in obtaining weapons and planning the bombing, Fortier said he never believed his buddy would actually carry out the attack. At his sentencing, Fortier made an emotional plea for forgiveness and apologized to the victims' families for not reporting the plot to police.

McVeigh was convicted of conspiracy and murder. He was on death row at a federal penitentiary in Indiana as of August 2000.

Nichols was convicted of conspiracy and manslaughter and sentenced to life in prison. He apparently was at his Kansas home at the time of the bombing. Investigators believe Nichols's role was collaborating with McVeigh to plan the attack, stealing weapons and other items that could be sold to raise money for materials, assisting McVeigh with transporting the truck and getaway car to Oklahoma City, and helping make the bomb and load it into the rental truck.

Fortier ultimately pleaded guilty to failure to report the bombing plot to police. Combined with lesser charges of selling stolen firearms and committing perjury when originally questioned by the FBI, it brought him a 12-year prison sentence and $200,000 fine in 1998. His prison sentence is being served at an undisclosed facility; authorities are concerned for his safety.

The Oklahoma City tragedy will leave lifelong emotional scars in the minds of thousands of individuals. Families and friends of the victims will never see life in quite the same light. For many survivors and loved ones—and for the millions across America who watched the proceedings unfold—the work of the FBI and other agencies ultimately brought closure to one of the worst crimes on record.

♣   ♣   ♣

What, exactly, is the Federal Bureau of Investigation? And when does it bring its powers to bear on a crime?

The FBI is the nation's best-known law enforcement agency at the federal level. Officially, it is one of the investigative agencies of the U.S. Department of Justice.

In essence, its mission is threefold: (1) to enforce federal (national) crime laws, (2) to protect America from foreign spies, and (3) to lead or help other law enforcement agencies, including town/city police departments, state agencies, other national agencies, and international entities.

Like other federal law enforcement organizations, such as the Central Intelligence Agency (CIA), the Secret Service, and the Bureau of Alcohol, Tobacco and Firearms, the FBI is mandated to perform specific functions. Some 260 federal laws are enforceable by the FBI. They cover wide-ranging matters. Examples include kidnapping, skyjacking, government corruption, civil rights violations, organized crime activities, bank robbery, interstate crimes, blackmail, drug trafficking, terrorism, copyright infringement, and many other types of wrongdoing. The FBI also gathers information about individuals and organizations that are potentially dangerous to the nation's security.

It is inaccurate to think of the FBI as the nation's "master" detective agency that steps in when a crime is too big or too difficult for local law enforcement

officials to handle. Instead, the FBI has been given responsibilities that complement, rather than override, state, county, and municipal police agencies. Its personnel often work with other police organizations as members of a team. The FBI's many specialists are regularly asked to assist in investigations led by local and state agencies.

Most murder cases, for instance, are handled by local or state law enforcement authorities. The FBI isn't called in unless or until such cases involve certain other crimes or become "interstate" in nature. For example, a string of small-store murders carried out in northern Illinois in 1981 did not involve the FBI until police had ample reason to suspect the same serial killer had committed a similar crime just across the state line

FBI officers escort Timothy McVeigh from a courthouse in Oklahoma. The FBI also prosecuted McVeigh's accomplices, Terry Nichols and Michael Fortier, whose testimonies helped convict McVeigh in the 1997 trial.

in Wisconsin. Through the FBI's police work in that case, Raymond Lee Stewart was eventually traced, apprehended, convicted, and executed.

A decade later, a sniper carried out a series of murders and attempted murders in rural southern Ohio. At first, various county sheriff's departments were investigating each incident as a single, unlinked crime. The investigative powers of the FBI were brought to bear on the case only after one of the crimes was committed on federal property.

Likewise, the famous bank robber John Dillinger in the 1930s was involved in many holdups over a period of months before FBI agents could officially be called in. When they were, it was not to chase Dillinger the bank robber; it was to apprehend Dillinger the car thief who had crossed state lines. Dillinger had escaped from an Indiana jail and fled in a stolen car to Chicago, Illinois.

The assassination of President John F. Kennedy in November 1963 was not technically a federal crime—although Kennedy's successor, President Lyndon B. Johnson, authorized the FBI to investigate. It wasn't until later that Congress officially placed the investigation of crimes against the American president in the hands of federal authorities.

A series of laws during the 20th century gave law enforcement agencies greater liberty to bring the FBI's resources to bear on crime solving. One example is the Interstate Transportation in Aid of Racketeering Law. It's now a federal matter not only to travel across state lines in committing certain crimes, but to use the phone or other communications media in those acts.

At the international level, the bureau is frequently asked to help investigate many types of criminal situations involving foreign citizens. The government must be careful how the FBI is deployed in these instances, since involvement can easily lead to political complications. For example, in November 1999, an EgyptAir

flight plunged into the Atlantic Ocean off the New England coast, killing everyone aboard. Early in the probe of flight data and voice recorders, investigators theorized that one of the copilots may have deliberately forced the jetliner into a death dive. At that point, the FBI was called in to investigate what was no longer believed to be a tragic accident, but possibly a mass crime. This development was not warmly received by the Egyptian government or by the family and friends of the suspected copilot.

The Federal Bureau of Investigation undertakes seven broad programs of investigation:

◆ *Applications for sensitive government positions.* Candidates for highly classified jobs must have exceptionally positive backgrounds. These include persons being considered for jobs with the Department of Justice, the White House staff, the Department of Energy, the Nuclear Regulatory Commission, and

For months after TWA Flight 800 crashed mysteriously in July 1996, investigators were unable to determine the cause of the crash. Eventually, the FBI and the National Transportation Safety Board pieced together the remains of the aircraft in an effort to figure out what went wrong. In 1997 the FBI concluded that the crash was not the result of a criminal act or a terrorist bomb. Three years later, Flight 800 was determined to have crashed because of an explosion in a fuel cell.

the federal courts. FBI agents thoroughly examine the applicants' personal, educational, and career records. They interview individuals who have known the applicant through the years.

◆ *Civil rights matters.* As enforcers of civil rights–related laws, FBI agents keep close watch on known and secret "hate" groups. They have had to investigate the activities of political extremist organizations on all sides of civil rights issues. Their work in this program involves not just violent acts and threats, but any infringement of civil rights laws. For instance, certain violations of hiring and housing statutes may warrant investigation by the FBI.

◆ *Counterterrorism.* The FBI must investigate and prevent, if possible, acts of terrorism and the taking of hostages inside the United States. The bureau is responsible for protecting foreign government

Other Federal Law Enforcement Agencies

The FBI is not the only federal law enforcement bureau. Some of the other federal law enforcement agencies include the Central Intelligence Agency (CIA), the Bureau of Alcohol, Tobacco and Firearms (ATF), the Secret Service, and the United States Coast Guard.

People generally think of the CIA as America's "international" law enforcement agency, although it is literally an "intelligence"—or information-gathering—agency. The CIA is involved in espionage and counterespionage and in keeping an eye on worldwide political situations that might affect the United States. In its role of gathering intelligence, it necessarily uses undercover means to obtain sensitive information concerning foreign countries' military strengths and activities, as well as the activities of possible foreign agents in this country. The CIA comes directly under the authority of the president and the National Security Council.

Agents of the Bureau of Alcohol, Tobacco and Firearms are often in the news thanks to their investigations of bombings, terrorism, distributors of illegal substances (such as drugs), and gang activities.

The Secret Service's most visible task is to protect members of the executive branch of government. These include the president, vice president, president-elect, vice president-elect, former presidents, and their families. Curiously, the Secret Service—America's oldest government law enforcement agency—was founded in 1865 to fight counterfeiting. It was not charged with presidential protection until after the assassination of President William McKinley in 1901. The officials and their guests in this country. And if a host country agrees, the FBI can investigate or assist in the probes of criminal acts involving American citizens abroad.

◆ *Foreign counterintelligence*. A related program involves countering the efforts of spies working in this country on behalf of governments or organizations considered hostile to the U.S. government. Some of these foreign agents represent powers known or suspected to condone or coordinate terrorist acts.

◆ *Financial crimes and corruption investigations*. We usually think of white-collar crimes like embezzlement and bank fraud when considering misdeeds in the world of finance. The FBI also investigates environmental crimes and health care fraud. Corruption in government and voting infractions come under FBI purview, as well.

agency today, as then, operates under the authority of the U.S. Treasury Department.

Although the U. S. Coast Guard is more often thought of as a branch of the military than a law enforcement agency, it is both. Unlike the army, navy, marines, and air force, the Coast Guard is among the 10 federal agencies with full police powers. Originally under the authority of the Treasury Department, the Coast Guard is now directed by the Department of Transportation, not the Department of Defense like other military branches.

In many cases the FBI works in conjunction with local police and other federal agencies. Here a police officer, an ATF agent, and an FBI agent search for evidence of a pipe bomb that exploded during the 1996 Summer Olympic Games in Atlanta.

- *Organized crime and narcotics.* Drug rings, illegal gambling, racketeering (extorting money through threats, bribes, etc.), and similar problems are in this category of investigation.
- *Violent crimes and major offenders.* This program covers a broad array of crimes, including the types that usually come to mind when we think of the FBI. Bank robberies and certain other types of theft; kidnappings; attacks against the president, vice president, or members of Congress; sexual exploitation of minors; crimes committed aboard airplanes—all come under this category of investigation. Crimes committed on government property, including Native American reservations, are included, as are crimes involving the interstate transportation of stolen items. The program also oversees searches for federal fugitives, escapees, and parole violators.

Over the years, local and state law enforcement agencies have increasingly turned to the Federal Bureau of Investigation for its training programs and vast resources. For example, police departments around the country today are networked via computer with the bureau's National Crime Information Center (NCIC). The NCIC maintains data concerning wanted and missing persons and stolen property nationwide; it is also linked to law enforcement agencies in Canada and Puerto Rico. More than 20 million records are stored in the NCIC's computer system, and the center processes more than 600,000 inquiries each day.

Another invaluable service the FBI provides in America's war on crime is maintaining the *Uniform Crime Reports.* Many—probably most—of the crime statistics you hear reported by the news media are based on these regularly updated records. Each month, local and state law enforcement agencies submit information to the FBI about the crimes committed in their cities, counties, and states. By compiling and analyzing these data, FBI crime fighters constantly keep a "finger on the pulse" of criminal trends. Among other benefits, this kind of reporting can suggest which kinds of crime prevention efforts are working and which geographic areas might benefit from specific types of law enforcement assistance.

Because of the scope of the bureau's records, facilities, and human resources, law enforcement agencies worldwide turn to the Federal Bureau of Investigation for assistance in combating crime. However, it's important to bear in mind that while the world looks to America's FBI for its impressive example and its diverse resources, the bureau is by no means a perfect crime-fighting force. Throughout its history, it has been criticized for mistakes—occasionally, for outright blunders. Its longtime director J. Edgar Hoover was accused of invading privacy and trampling the rights of certain individuals. Other bureau leaders and agents have come under similar fire. The bureau has also been perceived as a tool used by certain government leaders for personal purposes. For instance, a number of U.S. presidents—both Democratic and Republican—allegedly ordered Hoover and his agents to obtain information about the drinking habits and other personal vices of their political opponents.

By its very nature, the FBI holds enormous powers of investigation. This creates a state of constant tension. A free nation needs effective federal law enforcement—but it cannot tolerate unjustified invasions of privacy or violations of citizens' rights. FBI agents must walk a difficult, narrow path.

The FBI's
First Decades

Every organization has a beginning. How, you may be wondering, did the FBI come to be created? How long has it served as America's premier law enforcement agency? And how did we combat "federal" crimes before there was a Federal Bureau of Investigation?

Early America had no police officers, per se, but rather village "watchmen." This was based on the law enforcement system of England. It wasn't until 1845 that New York City established its official city "police force." Other cities followed New York's example.

By and large, the nation's first police officers received little or no training before beginning their duties. They learned by experience, on the street. Being notoriously underpaid for the often hazardous work they performed, they were easily susceptible to bribes and manipulation by members of the underworld and local political bosses.

In rural areas, law enforcement naturally took a

J. Edgar Hoover stands before a map that shows the national distribution of FBI officers. As FBI director for almost half a century, Hoover became a well-known public figure who both thrilled and enraged Americans with his innovative, yet controversial, approaches to law enforcement.

It was not until the mid-1800s that Americans saw a need for law enforcement beyond the town or city. The first state law enforcement organization was the Texas Rangers (above), who were legendary both for their equestrian skills and for their hard-nosed stance against outlaws.

different course. Sheriffs became the principal enforcers in the South and, as the nation expanded, in the West. In frontier towns, their efforts were aided by the appointment of town marshals.

On a larger scale, the Texas Rangers became the first state law enforcement organization in the mid-1800s. As the name implies, they originally operated on the open range, protecting settlers from hostile Indians and apprehending frontier criminals. They learned tracking and equestrian skills from Native Americans and became famous for their courage, doggedness, and rugged efficiency. During the 1870s, more than 400 rangers were in the field, purging the state of rampant lawlessness. Today the Texas Rangers are still at work, though the agency is much smaller and more specialized than in frontier days.

Charles J. Bonaparte was the U.S. attorney general under President Theodore Roosevelt in 1908. Both the president and the nation's chief prosecutor believed the United States needed an organized, progressive crime-fighting agency with expert investigators. Until that year, Bonaparte had been "borrowing" detectives from the Secret Service or hiring private investigators whenever his Department of Justice (DOJ) needed to investigate the mostly financial crimes that fell under its control.

Now, Bonaparte felt, it was time for his Department of Justice to have its own dedicated body of law enforcers. He wanted to have control over their work. Secret Service agents performed well when he needed them, but even when working on DOJ matters, they answered to their own agency chief. Besides, in May 1908, his practice of borrowing Secret Servicemen was forbidden by a new federal law. So Bonaparte felt a DOJ investigative agency had become not only desirable, but necessary.

Bonaparte formed a corps of ex-Secret Servicemen and other detectives. These individuals joined the Department of Justice's staff of "examiners," professional accountants who made sure Department of Justice finances were in order. Bonaparte, as attorney general, was their "director," although the 34 agents would report directly to Stanley W. Finch, the DOJ's chief examiner. The arrangement became official July 26, 1908.

The following year, Bonaparte was succeeded as attorney general by George Wickersham. The new attorney general named his detective unit simply the Bureau of Investigation; the DOJ's chief examiner came to be called "chief of the Bureau of Investigation"—the forerunner of today's FBI director.

The tiny new organization was a far cry from today's FBI. There was no training academy or even a training program; agents worked only with the experience and education they had acquired as detectives and/or accountants. Very few crimes came under their jurisdiction. But the agency was destined to grow as the federal government saw an increasing need for a crime-fighting force of this nature.

In fact, growth began almost immediately. In 1910, Congress passed the Mann Act, which made it a federal crime for prostitutes to be transported across state lines. The law did much more than allow the new bureau to investigate prostitution rings. Since many criminals were known to be involved with prostitutes, the Mann Act made it possible for the bureau to investigate the activities of these wanted men, who were trying to avoid state and local law enforcement agencies.

Several hundred agents and as many more staff sup-porters were added to the bureau. By that time, field offices were operating across the country. And the bureau's work soon broadened from its original finan-cial probes to include intelligence gathering and anti-smuggling activities. These new areas of authority were granted so the FBI could deal with increasing problems beginning in 1910 with the Mexican revolution just across our southern border and, later in the decade, with America's role in World War I.

In 1919, the bureau was given its most important expansion of power up to that point: the National Motor Vehicle Theft Act, charging the bureau with investigating interstate transportation of stolen cars. This permitted federal agents to help catch many types of criminals, including some of the nation's most dan-gerous individuals.

Many of those dangerous individuals lived during America's notorious "gangster era," which coincided almost exactly with the period of Prohibition (1920–33). Prohibition was the national banning of alcoholic beverages (specifically, of drinks containing more than 0.5 percent alcohol).

Why did a ban on booze result in one of the blood-iest eras of crime in the nation's history? Because it incited an underworld struggle for power and riches. Many Americans had no intention of letting Prohibition stop them from drinking alcohol. For suppliers and distributors willing to flout the new law, Prohibition produced a new way for big money to be made . . . illegally.

Drinking had been an issue in American social life and politics since the early 1800s. Historians have calculated that Americans were comparatively heavy drinkers during the first half of the 19th century. On the average, each citizen was drinking the equivalent of about 40 gallons of wine or 70 gallons of beer per year. The problems of alcoholism were obvious: most notably, lost productivity and family poverty.

By the time of the Civil War, "temperance" movements had succeeded in having the use of alcohol reduced ("tempered") or banned by law in some states. From then until the turn of the 20th century, a national temperance movement gained strength. The famous Women's Christian Temperance Union was formed in 1874, and similar societies followed. There was even a Prohibition Party, and its candidates vied for political office.

It wasn't until World War I, however, that the movement gained broad-based popular support. Congress in 1917 approved the Eighteenth Amendment to the Constitution. This edict banned the making, selling, or transporting of alcoholic beverages. The amendment was ratified by the states and took effect in 1920—and Bureau of Investigation agents, along with state and local police agents, quickly found themselves caught up in dangerous efforts to enforce the new law.

The Prohibition "experiment," as some have called

During the period of American history known as Prohibition (1920–33), the federal government turned to the FBI to clamp down on "bootleg" alcohol and to arrest the infamous gangsters that provided it. In this photo, FBI officials sort through an illicit cargo of whiskey.

it, was destined to fail. Many Americans took to brewing beer, fermenting wine, and distilling whiskey at home. Crude liquor stills became common in remote—and not-so-remote—rural areas. While these violations were subject to police raids, the far more ominous problem for law enforcement officers was the rapid rise in gang warfare.

Liquor was being smuggled into and across the country by ship, truck, and rail. Powerful gangs arose in major cities like Chicago, Boston, and New York and fought for control of smuggling and distribution channels, which were generating millions of dollars in illegal liquor sales.

The Bureau of Investigation was not specifically authorized to investigate illegal bootlegging. That task came under the jurisdictions of local law enforcement agencies and the U.S. Treasury Department, not the DOJ. However, the gangsters often broke laws that did fall under the DOJ's purview—such as interstate flight in stolen vehicles.

Gangsterism grew worse and wilder after the stock market crash of October 1929 sent America reeling into the Great Depression. Joblessness has always bred lawlessness, and the results of the Depression were predictable. Since many Americans viewed banks and other institutions as the cause of the country's economic woes, jobless individuals who became bank robbers were regarded as folk heroes. This placed bureau agents at a disadvantage in trying to identify and locate fugitives, who were often aided and hidden by sympathetic citizens. Luckily, agents received help from Congress. The legislators passed laws that added kidnapping and many other crimes to the list of federal offenses. They also—after more than two decades of investigations by the bureau—passed a belated law authorizing agents to carry guns and arrest criminal suspects.

More valuable to the bureau than congressional assistance, though, was strong leadership. This came—

for the first time since the bureau was formed—in 1924 in the person of a young, no-nonsense director: John Edgar Hoover. "J. Edgar," his preferred name, became almost synonymous with "FBI" during his half century as director. Hoover was loathed by criminals, feared by government officials and private citizens, and respected (though in some instances disliked) by the agents and staff who served under him. Especially after his death, he was widely criticized for heavy-handed and unethical—even illegal, at times—tactics and questionable political manipulation. He is reported to have dredged up unsavory information about the lives of certain officeholders (including U.S. presidents) and other public figures, supposedly using that information to exert power in Washington. On the other hand, he is roundly credited with building the bureau into an effective crime-fighting organization. And he was unquestionably the most famous "G-man" ("Government man," a popular nickname for an agent during the gangster era) of the 20th century.

Hoover was born in Washington, D.C. He took night classes while supporting himself by working as a clerk at the Library of Congress, and in 1917 he graduated from George Washington University Law School.

That was the year America entered World War I. Hoover went to work for the Department of Justice. After working as a file examiner, he was assigned to investigate suspected communists and other "subversives"—individuals working against the U.S. government. The attorney general at the time was A. Mitchell Palmer. Hoover's investigations, known as the "Palmer Raids," led to the deportation of many recent immigrants believed to be communists or communist sympathizers.

The "Palmer Raids" came under negative scrutiny. Here again arose the tension between the need to protect American democracy from subversion and the insistence that all U.S. citizens—even those who oppose the government—be granted freedom of expression. Hoover and Palmer were caught in the middle. At this moment in history, they leaned toward protecting the government, even if it meant deporting suspected subversives based on charges that weren't absolutely proven.

William J. Burns, who became director of the Bureau of Investigation in 1921, appointed Hoover as his assistant director. When Harlan Fiske Stone was chosen as U.S. attorney general by President Calvin Coolidge, Stone sought a "progressive" individual to lead the Bureau of Investigation. Hoover was his man. The young assistant became acting director in May 1924 and permanent director the following December.

One of his first actions as director was to dismiss agents he thought were poorly qualified. The seniority system had been used in promoting personnel at the bureau, which by then had more than 400 investigators and 200 support staff. Hoover realized this policy was shackling the bureau with lethargic, corrupt leadership and mediocre performance. His new structure called for across-the-board performance reviews. To join Hoover's Bureau of Investigation and remain there, current and aspiring agents soon learned they must work hard and constantly strive to better their skills. Regular inspections of the main and field offices were initiated. Under Hoover, being a Bureau of Investigation agent would be no cushy job.

Yet, Hoover's stringent requirements did not discourage young individuals interested in law enforcement careers. On the contrary, within a few years the Bureau of Investigation became the ultimate vocational goal of police officers. If you were accepted into the bureau, you had joined America's law enforcement elite.

Hoover, himself a lawyer, preferred to enlist agent trainees who had either law or accounting degrees (credentials that still are considered favorable among applicants). Such credentials weren't enough for Hoover, however; where few police or sheriff departments provided formal training for their officers, Hoover set his agents apart by instituting a formal instruction course.

In 1935—the same year the bureau officially became the Federal Bureau of Investigation—he established what is now the world-famous FBI Academy in Quantico, Virginia. Within several years, law enforcement agencies across the country were sending officers there for special training in criminal investigation.

In addition to their training, FBI agents literally had to "go by the book." Besides understanding the basics of criminal law and the legal process, they had to follow an internal manual of bureau rules and procedures.

Hoover also began organizing a central body of criminal information that would benefit not just his bureau but also local law enforcement agencies. He urged Congress to place the nation's largest banks of fingerprint records under his bureau's Identification

Under J. Edgar Hoover's direction, the FBI soon earned a reputation for its rigorous training program. FBI trainees learned how to closely examine evidence, as seen in this 1933 photograph.

Division. In 1926, local police agencies began sending criminals' fingerprint cards to bureau headquarters in Washington, D.C. The FBI Identification Division's fingerprint collection would eventually become the largest such collection in the world.

While thus strengthening his agency on the inside, Hoover set to work on the outside. He wanted the bureau—which was still fairly obscure—to become well known and respected across America. Image, he believed, would be priceless in the fight against crime, as public sentiment and shelter often went to the criminals. Hoover asserted that "the real problem of law enforcement is in trying to obtain the cooperation and sympathy of the public."

Beginning in the early 1930s, Hoover began an ongoing campaign to publicize the work of his agents and his bureau in their fight against the rising tide of crime. He developed a rapport with the major newspapers of the day as well as with the era's two new media sensations: radio and motion pictures. Still, many an American youngster in make-believe games chose to be a famous bank robber like John Dillinger instead of the G-man.

John Dillinger—popularly (but not officially) depicted as "public enemy number one"—was a household name in the 1930s. His criminal bent may have begun in childhood. Although he was raised in a middle-class home in Indianapolis, Indiana, his mother died when he was three years old, and he matured under the heavy hand of a stern father and a hated stepmother. As a teenager, he began to run wild, dropping out of school and frequently enjoying the nightlife with friends until morning. He apparently committed at least one crime—an auto theft—before the age of 20, but the victim did not press charges.

After joining but quickly deserting the navy, Dillinger was arrested and convicted in 1924 for attempted robbery in Indiana. The 2- to 20-year sentence was unusually harsh. Bitter, Dillinger made several escape attempts within the first few months of his incarceration but these were unsuccessful. During his nine years of imprisonment, he became vengeful and, arguably, incorrigible—unable to become a law-abiding citizen. By the time he was released on parole in May 1933, he had served extended time for gambling, disorderly conduct, and destroying state property while in prison.

Within a month, Dillinger began committing store and bank robberies. He was arrested in September 1933 but soon escaped from the Lima, Ohio, jail with the help of several former prison buddies. They began a three-month crime spree that eventually took them to Arizona. There, Dillinger and three others were arrested after firemen recognized them while responding to a hotel blaze. Several law enforcement officers had been killed during their rampages in Illinois, Indiana, and Ohio, and Dillinger was taken to the Crown Point, Indiana, jail to await trial for murder.

It was there that he performed perhaps his most notorious act: bolting from the legendary "escape-proof" Crown Point jail. With a fake pistol whittled from wood or soap and blackened with boot polish, Dillinger surprised his guards, compelled them to let him out of his cell, armed himself with two machine guns, and took off in the county sheriff's car.

So far, Dillinger had done nothing to warrant pursuit by the Bureau of Investigation. The robberies, escapes, and even killings had been local and state offenses. But while fleeing from Crown Point, he crossed the state line into Illinois in the stolen car, en route to Chicago. This violated a federal law: the National Motor Vehicle Theft Act. J. Edgar Hoover's G-men now had reason to focus their midwestern resources on the famous desperado.

Like historical outlaws such as Jesse James and Billy the Kid, Dillinger had become a hero in the minds of

Crime fighters had their hands full in the 1920s and 1930s, the heyday of gangsters. No criminal seemed as indomitable as the popularly nicknamed "Public Enemy Number One": John Dillinger, posing above with a pistol and sub-machine gun. Dillinger was a national menace for 10 years, but his crime spree ended in 1934 when he was killed in a shoot-out with federal agents.

many penniless, desperate Americans. They had lost everything in the Depression. By robbing banks, Dillinger and other bank robbers in the 1930s seemed to be striking a blow for the downtrodden—although their main objective was to stuff their own wallets.

Forming a new gang in St. Paul, Minnesota, Dillinger robbed more banks during the spring of 1934. In late April, Dillinger and some of his cronies were secluded at a lake lodge called Little Bohemia near Rhinelander, Wisconsin. Bureau of Investigation agents led by Chicago bureau chief Melvin Purvis, acting on a tip, arrived one night and surrounded the building. Tragically, several unsuspecting lodgers were hit in the ensuing gunfire—while the criminals escaped along the lakeshore.

Three months later, Purvis and Special Agent Samuel Cowley, who had been assigned to lead the Dillinger investigation, were approached by an informant in Chicago. She was a Romanian national named Ana Cumpanas, operator of a brothel in nearby Gary, Indiana. Cumpanas went by the alias "Anna Sage," and she would go down in criminal history as the famous "Lady in Red" for her role in the apparent shooting of Dillinger.

Cumpanas told the agents that Dillinger had regularly been seeing one of the prostitutes at her establishment. In fact, Cumpanas was to accompany Dillinger and his girlfriend to a movie the following night. She promised to wear a bright red dress so officers could easily identify the trio.

Why would she betray her client? Primarily because she faced the threat of deportation to her home country—an undesirable place to be, with the rise of Hitler's Nazi regime in nearby Germany. She also wanted a cash reward.

As planned, Dillinger attended the movie *Manhattan Melodrama* with the two women at Chicago's Biograph Theater. As they exited the lobby about 10:30 P.M. on

July 22, Purvis, Cowley, and their agents were posted along the street. Dillinger obviously sensed a trap; he began running down an alley, drawing a pistol. Shots rang out. Dillinger fell to his face in the side street, hit by three bullets. He died within minutes.

Ever since that day, a question has persisted: was Dillinger really apprehended? Some historians argue that the man shot and identified as Dillinger was a look-alike. One author has suggested the imposter was a Chicago criminal named James Lawrence and that he was part of a conspiracy to take the heat off Dillinger by tricking law enforcement officials into believing he was dead. Cumpanas, it is argued, was one of the plotters, as was at least one Chicago police detective who helped arrange her meeting with the Bureau of Investigation.

The agency, however, considered the case closed. Unquestionably, the Dillinger gang's reign of terror was over. Ana Cumpanas was eventually deported to Europe.

The FBI was becoming a formidable crime-fighting force. By 1936, most of the famous gangsters, from Dillinger to Bonnie and Clyde to Al Capone, had been captured or slain in battles with law enforcement officers. Hoover's strategy was starting to pay dividends: the FBI had become symbolic of crime fighting in the minds of most Americans.

J. Edgar Hoover F.B.I. Building

THE FBI
MATURES

Gangsters weren't the only wrongdoers the Federal Bureau of Investigation dealt with during Prohibition. As enforcers of our civil rights policies, the FBI spent much time investigating the activities of the Ku Klux Klan. A number of Klan leaders and operatives were arrested for their activities against African Americans. The FBI also investigated violence brought on by labor unrest.

During the 1930s, the FBI was also called on to monitor the activities of the American offshoots of European political movements considered dangerous to national security. Most notable were the Fascists (Italy), Nazis (Germany), and Communists (Russia). In 1940, with World War II already ravaging Europe, Congress passed an act banning subversive organizations—those working to overthrow the U.S. government from within. FBI probes of political threats broadened.

World War II brought a new and dramatic set of concerns for the American government. Besides investigating antigovernment political movements, the FBI had to turn its attention to the crimes of espionage (international spying) and sabotage (deliberately destroying property and lives in an effort to gain military advantage). Foreign agents of every major nation were active on all fronts of the war in Europe, and by the 1930s Nazi and Communist operatives were already gathering intelligence inside the United States.

A further threat came from the Pacific. Japan—the nation that would ultimately provoke America into the war with its surprise bombardment of Pearl Harbor—used spies to learn what it could about U.S. military defenses and industrial capacities.

After the war, investigating espionage and subversive activities would be turned over to the newly organized Central Intelligence Agency (CIA). For the present, though, the FBI trained special agents to focus on these security issues. New field agents were also recruited and put through a shortened training program; the bureau's employee rolls almost doubled to more than 13,000. In addition, the bureau engaged American scientists, engineers, and other professionals to help address special security concerns posed by the world war.

Their efforts paid off in the early 1940s with the breakup of a major spy ring and the capture of German saboteurs who'd arrived on the East Coast aboard a U-boat (a German submarine). Soon, concerned about the high number of German- and Japanese-born citizens living in South America, President Franklin D. Roosevelt designated a special group of FBI agents to investigate wartime activities on that neighboring continent. The unit was called the Special Intelligence Service.

As the nation scrambled to prepare itself for war after the Pearl Harbor strike, German and Japanese Americans suspected of anti-American sympathies were questioned by the FBI and other government authorities. America's treatment of certain foreign-born citizens came under criticism after the war. Many Japanese Americans (including some who wholly supported the American cause during World War II) were confined to closely guarded camp cities. But during those years of uncertainty, suspicion, and fear of invasion and bombardment, those procedures were generally accepted by the government and the public as necessary security measures.

After Germany's defeat in World War II, communistic Russia and the democratic United States became the world's foremost powers—and both quickly developed nuclear arms programs. Thus began the period of the Cold War, in which tension between the Soviet Union and the United States dominated world politics for nearly a half-century. Security matters during this Cold War era naturally involved the FBI. Besides performing background security checks for government agencies, the bureau looked into security matters concerning the White House. Fear of Soviet operatives meant that Communist or "left wing" groups and individuals in America came under close scrutiny.

U.S. fears were prompted when Russian leader Joseph Stalin, soon after the war ended, declared that communism must replace capitalism as an economic system. Stalin predicted that future wars would decide the issue. By then, the FBI and other agencies were already investigating the theft of classified government documents and attempts to steal atomic weapon secrets. When the Soviet Union developed its own version of the atomic bomb in 1949, U.S. security intensified at all levels of government.

The FBI, sometimes under direct order from the White House, had been investigating spy and terrorist activities for 30 years before the Cold War began. In 1946, the Atomic Energy Act required the FBI to determine the loyalty of government workers who had access to sensitive nuclear energy information. Presidents Harry S. Truman and Dwight D. Eisenhower broadened the FBI's role to include investigations of any federal employee suspected of disloyalty. A number of alleged spies were arrested and convicted.

The government's fervor for rooting out Communists reached new heights in the 1950s, when Senator Joseph R. McCarthy—with the FBI's help—led a sensational campaign against scores of government officials, journalists, and entertainment celebrities. Although the charges could never be proved, many reputations were tarnished. The "McCarthy era" is cited as perhaps the worst example of governmental abuse of power in American history.

During the 1960s, the bureau began devoting increased attention to civil rights violations. At issue, primarily, were the rights of African Americans and other minorities to have equal access to restaurants, hotels, and other public facilities; to vote; to attend traditionally all-white schools; to serve on juries; etc.

Previously, civil rights laws had permitted federal investigations only in rare cases. But in 1964, after three voter registration workers were killed in Mississippi, the U.S. Department of Justice placed the investigation in the hands of the FBI. Seven men were eventually convicted in the murders. A 1966 Supreme Court decision reinforced federal jurisdiction in civil rights cases.

These new responsibilities did not displace the FBI's attention to an old, familiar enemy: organized crime. Although America's infamous gangster era had ended with the repeal of Prohibition in the 1930s, organized crime was far from defeated. Investigators in 1957 identified La Cosa Nostra, or "the mafia," as a national crime syndicate. Congress strengthened federal gambling and racketeering laws. FBI agents and other investigators were able to ensure the convictions of many major crime bosses.

In the 1970s, organized crime tightened its grip on illegal drug traffic—a problem that quickly became more

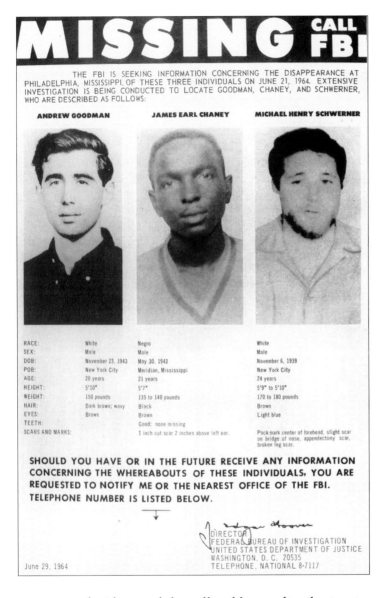

MISSING CALL FBI

THE FBI IS SEEKING INFORMATION CONCERNING THE DISAPPEARANCE AT PHILADELPHIA, MISSISSIPPI, OF THESE THREE INDIVIDUALS ON JUNE 21, 1964. EXTENSIVE INVESTIGATION IS BEING CONDUCTED TO LOCATE GOODMAN, CHANEY, AND SCHWERNER, WHO ARE DESCRIBED AS FOLLOWS:

ANDREW GOODMAN **JAMES EARL CHANEY** **MICHAEL HENRY SCHWERNER**

RACE:	White	Negro	White
SEX:	Male	Male	Male
DOB:	November 23, 1943	May 30, 1943	November 6, 1939
POB:	New York City	Meridian, Mississippi	New York City
AGE:	20 years	21 years	24 years
HEIGHT:	5'10"	5'7"	5'9" to 5'10"
WEIGHT:	150 pounds	135 to 140 pounds	170 to 180 pounds
HAIR:	Dark brown; wavy	Black	Brown
EYES:	Brown	Brown	Light blue
TEETH:		Good; none missing	
SCARS AND MARKS:		1 inch cut scar 2 inches above left ear.	Pock mark center of forehead, slight scar on bridge of nose, appendectomy scar, broken leg scar.

SHOULD YOU HAVE OR IN THE FUTURE RECEIVE ANY INFORMATION CONCERNING THE WHEREABOUTS OF THESE INDIVIDUALS, YOU ARE REQUESTED TO NOTIFY ME OR THE NEAREST OFFICE OF THE FBI. TELEPHONE NUMBER IS LISTED BELOW.

DIRECTOR
FEDERAL BUREAU OF INVESTIGATION
UNITED STATES DEPARTMENT OF JUSTICE
WASHINGTON, D. C. 20535
TELEPHONE, NATIONAL 8-7117

June 29, 1964

In 1964 the FBI investigated the brutal murders of three civil rights workers in Mississippi. This investigation marked the beginning of the FBI's involvement in civil rights cases. Two years later the Supreme Court granted jurisdiction to the FBI in all civil rights cases.

sinister and widespread than illegal liquor distribution in the 1920s and early 1930s. In 1982, the FBI was given joint jurisdiction with the federal Drug Enforcement Administration to investigate narcotics crimes.

The 1960s and 1970s were the era of the Vietnam War. Protests against U.S. involvement in Vietnam brought unprecedented social unrest to the nation's streets and college campuses. Property damage and confrontations with police were everyday occurrences. Some 3,000 bombings (and 50,000 bomb threats) occurred in the United States in 1970, many of them related to the antiwar movement. Since the movement was ultimately directed against the U.S. government, the FBI was constantly engaged in war-related investigations at home. The bureau's actions, such as undercover infiltration of protest groups, were sometimes seen as infringements against the guaranteed rights of protesting citizens. Once more, the FBI was caught in the conflicting role of protecting the United States government while also protecting the rights of individuals who believed they should criticize the government.

In May 1972, longtime director J. Edgar Hoover died in his sleep. He was 77 years old. Richard Nixon was president. Hoover had headed the bureau for eight presidential administrations and served under 18 attorney generals during a half century when the nature of crime—and crime fighting—changed dramatically.

After his death, Hoover's career would spark endless controversy. In his writings, Hoover stated that the FBI should be employed "to ensure that no citizen is deprived of the free exercise or enjoyment of any right or privilege secured . . . by the Constitution." Many critics, however, believe the director was guilty of trampling the rights and privileges he claimed to defend.

Hoover deployed his bureau to support and defend what he considered the American ideal, and he disdained radicals on all sides of social issues. For example, he perceived communism as a threat to the American way of life, and thus challenged it, aiding Senator McCarthy in his communist witch-hunt in the 1950s. His scrutiny was directed to the extreme right, as well. FBI agents throughout the 20th century kept close watch over Ku Klux Klan activities and were instrumental in bringing Klan members to justice for civil rights crimes.

Ironically, Hoover also disliked civil rights activists. He suspected civil rights leader Dr. Martin Luther King Jr. of communistic influences. Over a period of years, agents conducted wiretaps and electronic surveillance of King's travels. Obtaining embarrassing information about King's private life, the FBI apparently used it in attempts to intimidate King and ruin his public image and credibility. Later, the bureau also investigated black militants, such as the leaders of the Black Panthers. Hoover's meddling was not limited to communism and civil rights, either. He also targeted political figures he disliked, seeking to undermine their power and effectiveness by "provoking scandal."

The antiwar movement of the 1960s and early 1970s had many violent outbreaks. Here, riot officers break up a sit-in at a chemical plant that produced napalm. In an attempt to prevent riots, J. Edgar Hoover ordered the FBI to infiltrate many protest organizations; in doing this, however, critics of Hoover and the organization claimed the protesters' constitutional rights were being trampled.

Within the bureau, Hoover was a stickler for rules and discipline. For example, he would not allow agents to drink coffee at their desks. The bureau's white-shirt-and-tie dress code was not to be varied. He even insisted that the acronym "FBI" always be written with periods: "F.B.I." Some agents regarded many of Hoover's minute requirements to be childish, and they privately resented the director.

Regardless of whether they appreciated his management style, however, virtually all agents respected him as the leader who shaped the FBI into the world's most effective law enforcement agency. Retired agent and author Phil Kerby, after mentioning examples of Hoover's odd directives, wrote in his book *With Honor and Purpose*:

> But how important are those things when you remember that Hoover created the FBI Academy, the greatest law enforcement school in the world? He launched the FBI lab, which in spite of criticism remains the gold standard for forensic science. He conceived the National Crime Information Center, a national computer linkup for law enforcement agencies, and then forced it through a leery Congress. . . . [Hoover] took a small, inept, and hopelessly corrupt agency and turned it into the planet's most powerful and professional police force.

Despite losing the driving force behind its half century of expansion in both power and prestige, the FBI remained America's premier law enforcement organization after Hoover's death. In the last quarter of the 20th century, the agency found itself dealing with an increase in certain violent crimes and in white-collar (financial) crimes. Those issues continue to challenge the FBI at the dawn of the 21st century. In addition, long-term FBI probes of corruption during the 1980s and 1990s resulted in convictions of government officials, judges, banking officials, "bad cops," and even congressional representatives.

With the dissolution of the Soviet Union on

Christmas Day 1991, Cold War tensions eased. The FBI immediately reassigned 300 of its counterintelligence agents to other types of criminal investigations. Today, organized crime, white-collar crime, foreign counterintelligence, and counterterrorism are the four priorities of the bureau.

How the FBI Operates

More than 11,000 men and women make up the Federal Bureau of Investigation. Some are based at agency headquarters in Washington, D.C. Others work at the 56 field offices and several hundred satellite offices around the country. Field offices may have any number of agents, from one in a small municipality to more than a thousand in cities like Los Angeles. The bureau also has more than 30 offices in major foreign countries, where agents serve as crime-fighting liaisons, advising the host nation's law enforcement officials. In addition, the bureau employs more than 16,000 support personnel.

No two work days are the same for FBI field agents. One agent, operating alone or with various combinations of partners, may be assigned to several—or dozens—of cases at once. Their most obvious

Police and FBI agents examine the area where two agents died in a bloody gun battle with robbery suspects.

assignments are to investigate reported crimes, collect and preserve evidence, and question witnesses and potential suspects. Agents perform searches of suspects' homes or offices as well as other facilities that may reveal evidence.

A time-consuming and often tedious part of the job is poring through many kinds of information, tracing and linking individuals and events via a "paper trail." Each record must be checked for accuracy. The information is digested and filed in reports.

Many agents develop relationships with confidential informants. These are individuals who are not suspected of participating in a crime but who may have important information about it. Informants may have obtained their knowledge of the crime from underworld contacts—sometimes through acquaintances or friendships with the person or persons directly involved. Although the details they share might be weak or inadmissible as courtroom evidence, they can be pivotal in pointing agents to a suspect, a key witness, or a piece of damning evidence. Some of these individuals, because of their underworld connections and specific kinds of knowledge, are far more valuable to investigators as informants than as witnesses at a trial.

At times, agents themselves go "undercover." Concealing their identities, they get to know criminals in order to gather evidence from the "inside." Sometimes they live and work with the criminals they're investigating, reporting secretly to their FBI colleagues. Undercover operations may last for months or years before the agents obtain the ironclad evidence they'll need to ensure successful prosecution of the case.

Undercover work is thrilling but extremely dangerous. If the underworld targets learn or even suspect an agent's true identity, not only does the operation fail, but the agent's life is in danger.

A safer means of gathering information is surveillance, often called a "stakeout." This typically involves spending hours in a parked car or another inconspicuous or unseen vantage point close to a suspect residence, workplace, or rendezvous. Agents on stakeout take care to blend in with the locals so that they don't stand out. They wear business suits, if they're in an office building or business district, and well-worn street clothes if in a low-rent neighborhood. This strategy of blending in is a fairly recent development. While today's bureau personnel are broadly diversified in race and gender, until the 1970s all agents were men, and almost all were Caucasian. They were notoriously obvious for their standard dress: dark slacks, white shirts, neckties, and close-cut hair. Veteran agents recall that this "FBI look" frequently worked against them while on stakeout or when communicating with informants "in the field."

The agents' surveillance assignment may be to apprehend a wanted fugitive if he or she appears. It may be to confront a reluctant individual for questioning. It may be simply to observe the activities of a suspect and those with whom the suspect comes into contact. Often it proves fruitless: agents may wait for hours on end, day after day, in all kinds of weather for a person who never appears or for an anticipated activity that never occurs. But this is the kind of routine "detective work" that is the backbone of criminal apprehension, evidence gathering, and, ultimately, case solving.

On occasion—sometimes when they least expect it—the boring tedium is suddenly shattered and the agents become players in a real-life action drama. An armed fugitive flees. A chase ensues. Death threatens the pursuing agents from around the next corner, inside a closed door or open window, within the dark recesses of a musty basement, from the branches of a shade tree. Each day, FBI agents around the country deal with dangerous individuals. Efficient SWAT teams and state-of-the-art weapons and defenses reduce the peril, but the risks can never be eliminated.

Perhaps the classic case of G-men in the line of fire occurred in 1934. The fugitive was "Baby Face Nelson," one of America's notorious criminals.

As a teenager in the early 1920s, running with the wrong crowd on the streets of Chicago, Lester Gillis tried to make it clear that he did not like being called "Baby Face." But because he looked younger than his years and never grew taller than five feet four inches tall, his cronies pinned the nickname on him and it stuck.

At age 14, Gillis was in reform school for stealing a car. He spent most of his teen years behind bars. In 1928, at age 20, he was a free man. Calling himself George Nelson, he got married, but he didn't settle down. Rather, he rose to more serious crimes: robbing banks and working for the mob as a strong-arm thug to force labor leaders and businessmen into cooperation.

In 1932, after serving a year in prison for robbery and facing a second charge, he escaped from guards who were transporting him from one prison to another. The nation was in for a crime spree of maniacal savagery.

At first the fugitive's criminal activities were relatively tame. He was hired by the underworld as a guard on a bootlegging truck in California. But soon he was on the move, working with different criminal partners. Authorities linked him with murders and other crimes as far afield as Minnesota, Illinois, Nebraska, and Nevada.

In 1934, Nelson joined the infamous John Dillinger gang in Chicago. Nelson fancied himself as Dillinger's equal—or superior. The young killer's brutal behavior surprised even Dillinger, who had just broken out of prison himself. On one occasion while the two were driving, Nelson reportedly ran a stop sign and hit an oncoming car. Nelson proceeded to shoot the angry motorist in the face for getting in his way.

During their bank holdups, Nelson was a raging demon, shooting not only guards and police but also unarmed bystanders. In Mason City, Iowa, Dillinger

Lester Gillis, better known as Baby Face Nelson, was an original member of John Dillinger's infamous gang. Nelson met the same fate as his former partner in a separate 1934 shootout with federal agents.

reportedly had to intervene to prevent Nelson from murdering a bank vice president.

Bureau of Investigation agents dispersed the Dillinger gang in a raid while the outlaws were in hiding at a Wisconsin lake lodge in April 1934. The gang escaped, but in the aftermath, Nelson killed a bureau agent and wounded two other lawmen as they approached to arrest him. He made off in the officers' car.

After Dillinger was slain by bureau agents three months later, Nelson continued his spree. In November 1934 near Barrington, Illinois, after a wild car chase,

Chicago FBI inspector Samuel Cowley and special agent Herman Hollis found themselves in a furious gun battle with Nelson. The fugitive, who was traveling with his wife and a crime partner, traded fire with the agents for several minutes. Then, according to the accounts of dumbfounded witnesses, he rose from his cover and walked toward the agents, machine gun blazing. Hollis was killed instantly in a spray of bullets; Cowley died the next morning of multiple gunshots.

But Nelson, too, was mortally wounded. He staggered to the agents' car and fled the scene with his accomplices. The next day, officials received a phone call telling them that a body could be found in a rural ditch. Stripped of his clothes by his companions—apparently to thwart identification—and dumped, Baby Face had 17 bullet wounds.

Most criminal investigations and apprehensions are more subtle. Rather than guns blazing in the street, such work involves painstaking gathering of evidence. Professional criminal investigators are thorough experts. Whereas civilians might visit a crime scene and locate, say, 10 clues, a team of law enforcement investigators will find hundreds. They take their time, work methodically, and "leave no stone unturned"—literally. In the end, most of the evidence they find and record may have little or no bearing on the eventual arrest and trial of the criminal, but it must all be collected and analyzed.

Seasoned detectives know that many details that at first appear insignificant can prove or disprove a suspect's involvement. Objects and arrangements that seem casual to the untrained eye may actually be anything but casual. At a murder scene, the placement and position of the body might look haphazard at first glance, but it can speak volumes to those who intimately understand the horrible patterns of homicide. For example, the way blood is splattered can help determine from which direction a bullet was fired.

Investigating a crime or event can sometimes force an agent to confront conflicting emotions; the desire to thoroughly investigate a crime scene can be at odds with the revulsion the aftermath of violent death can cause. Retired agent Phil Kerby, in his book *With Honor and Purpose*, recounted a grotesque, unexpected assignment he was given as a first-year agent in the Albany, New York, field office. After a plane crashed into a mountain, Kerby was sent with other agents to join special investigators from the bureau's Washington headquarters. Their mission: to begin identifying the charred, twisted bodies.

A morgue had been set up at a local hospital. One of the FBI Disaster Team technicians handed Kerby a pair of large clippers and told him to "go to work on the fingers." Dumbfounded, Kerby didn't understand at first that he was to cut off the victims' tightly clenched fingers so prints could be taken. When he realized the gruesome nature of the task, he couldn't bring himself to carry it out.

Veteran agents, sympathetic to his queasiness, assumed the duty and dismissed him for the day to recover his composure. But the next morning, while others continued laboring in the morgue, Kerby had to accompany an older agent to the home of one of the victims' families. This mission was even more difficult: gently break the news to the parents that their daughter had probably been aboard the doomed airplane, and lift fingerprints from her bedroom for positive identification. Dusting graphite around the young woman's hairbrush and other personal items, Kerby was forced to confront, at point-blank range, the heartrending reality that a promising life had been abruptly, brutally ended.

"On the way out," he wrote, "I saw tears trickling silently down the [mother's] cheeks. In the car, they ran down mine, too."

Agents not only have to be intelligent, determined, well-trained, and thorough, but they also have to be emotionally tough. They have to be able to face gruesome crime scenes without flinching and not allow their emotions to interfere with proper procedure. There is another requirement as well: discretion.

Ten Most Wanted Fugitives

Some of the fugitives currently on the "Ten Most Wanted Fugitives" list have been there only a few months. One has been wanted since 1981. As of August 2000, they included:

Suspect Name	Description	Reward
Ramon Eduardo Arellano-Felix	A 36-year-old leader of the "Tijuana Cartel," a drug ring with a violent record in importing controlled substances.	$50,000
Usama Bin Laden	A terrorist leader wanted for his backing of the 1998 bombings of U.S. embassies in Tanzania and Kenya. More than 200 people were killed in those apparently related terrorist attacks.	Up to $5 million
James J. Bulger	An organized crime figure in the Boston area suspected of extortion and RICO (racketeering) violations. Illegal gambling, drugs, and loan-sharking reputedly are parts of his "profession."	$1 million
Victor Manuel Gerena	A 41-year-old bank robber who made off with an estimated $7 million in a Connecticut heist.	$50,000
Glen Stewart Godwin	A convicted murderer at large after a prison escape.	$50,000
James Charles Kopp	A man accused of violating the Freedom of Access to Clinic Entrances Act, who allegedly was involved in the killing of a doctor.	Up to $50,000
Eric Robert Rudolph	The suspected bomber of a number of public and business sites at which a police officer died and more than 150 people were injured.	$1 million
Arthur Lee Washington Jr.	A militant ex-convict who fled after shooting a state highway patrol officer with a semiautomatic pistol.	$50,000
Donald Eugene Webb	A career criminal and "master of assumed identities" believed to have fled after beating and shooting a police chief.	$50,000

Law enforcement agencies and prosecutors are known for being tight-lipped about their investigations and criminal procedures. They have to be. Improper pretrial publicity can destroy a case against a known criminal.

The 10th fugitive on the list, Agustin Vasquez-Mendoza, a drug ring conspirator allegedly involved in the killing of an undercover federal drug enforcement agent, has been located.

FBI TEN MOST WANTED FUGITIVE

MURDER OF U.S. NATIONALS OUTSIDE THE UNITED STATES;
CONSPIRACY TO MURDER U.S. NATIONALS OUTSIDE THE UNITED STATES;
ATTACK ON A FEDERAL FACILITY RESULTING IN DEATH

USAMA BIN LADEN

Date of Photograph Unknown

Aliases: Usama Bin Muhammad Bin Ladin, Shaykh Usama Bin Ladin, the Prince, the Emir, Abu Abdallah, Mujahid Shaykh, Hajj, the Director

DESCRIPTION

Date of Birth:	1957	Hair:	Brown
Place of Birth:	Saudi Arabia	Eyes:	Brown
Height:	6' 4" to 6' 6"	Complexion:	Olive
Weight:	Approximately 160 pounds	Sex:	Male
Build:	Thin	Nationality:	Saudi Arabian
Occupation(s):	Unknown		
Remarks:	He is the leader of a terrorist organization known as Al-Qaeda "The Base." He walks with a cane.		

CAUTION

USAMA BIN LADEN IS WANTED IN CONNECTION WITH THE AUGUST 7, 1998, BOMBINGS OF THE UNITED STATES EMBASSIES IN DAR ES SALAAM, TANZANIA AND NAIROBI, KENYA. THESE ATTACKS KILLED OVER 200 PEOPLE.

CONSIDERED ARMED AND EXTREMELY DANGEROUS

IF YOU HAVE ANY INFORMATION CONCERNING THIS PERSON, PLEASE CONTACT YOUR LOCAL FBI OFFICE OR THE NEAREST U.S. EMBASSY OR CONSULATE.

REWARD

The United States Government is offering a reward of up to $5 million for information leading directly to the apprehension or conviction of Usama Bin Laden.

www.fbi.gov

Since 1949 the FBI has posted its list of the "Ten Most Wanted Fugitives," along with full descriptions of each fugitive, as seen above. As of August 2000, 430 of 459 "Most Wanted" fugitives have been apprehended.

At the same time, investigators rely heavily on the public to supply vital information. John Douglas, a former FBI criminal profiler and author of several books on criminal investigation, explains the balance investigators have to maintain. He writes: "My experience has shown me that the public is very often a critical partner with the police in bringing dangerous men to justice. So while it is often a good idea [for investigators] to withhold certain specific facts and pieces of information, my own bias is that you work with the media and let the public help you as much as possible."

Usually, when police go public in asking for information, they are inundated with far too many "clues." Almost all of them prove to be useless. But investigators welcome all information and sort through it patiently, considering each incidental report carefully before focusing on those that hold the greatest promise. Somewhere in the haystack of information, they know, may lurk the needle that will lead to solving the crime.

Gaining public cooperation was the very reason the FBI created its famous "most wanted list." One day in 1949, a reporter for a syndicated news service asked FBI sources to name the "toughest" fugitives the bureau was pursuing at the time. The agents complied. The resulting article was one of the most widely read pieces published nationwide that year. It inspired J. Edgar Hoover, the bureau's director, to create an official, ongoing "Ten Most Wanted Fugitives" list.

The stated purpose of the list is "to publicize particularly dangerous fugitives who might not otherwise merit nationwide attention." During its first 50 years, more than 430 "most wanted" individuals were arrested after citizens recognized them through posters and other media.

The FBI's 56 field offices recommend criminals to be added to the list. Two basic criteria determine which of the many fugitives in federal cases qualify as "most wanted": (1) a lengthy record of serious crimes that are especially threatening to society and (2) an absence of other publicity that might help lead to the person's arrest. Some suspects become widely recognizable after a particularly shocking crime, because their pictures are published in local newspapers and on TV news programs. The "most wanted," on the other hand, are chosen partly because their crimes—although they may have been just as serious as others—were less sensational and the suspects' identities were thus less publicized.

After the field offices identify "most wanted" prospects, the FBI's Criminal Investigative Division (CID) in Washington and, ultimately, the bureau's deputy director review each nominee's case and select those to be added to the top 10. A new fugitive will not be added until a current one is removed.

Most suspects are eventually caught. As of August 2000, approximately 430 of 459 fugitives named to the list during its half century of existence had been found. Occasionally, a person is removed from the list before being caught because other fugitives come to be considered even more "wanted." In rare instances, some or all charges are dropped against the individual.

Obviously, far more than 459 dangerous fugitives have been sought and caught by the FBI since 1949. The bureau regularly publishes new information concerning criminals not listed among the "Ten Most Wanted."

"Wanted" posters are commonly found at U.S. Post Offices and other public facilities. Television news programs and newspapers sometimes publish the "mug" photos of criminal suspects in sensational cases. By simply remembering the faces you see, you may one day find yourself in a position to serve as an FBI informant . . . and perform an important service for your community and society.

For a special breed of American citizens, "performing an important service" in the fight against crime leads to an interest in crime fighting as a career. This

Trainees practice their marks-manship on the rifle range at the FBI's training facility at Quantico, Virginia. Each of these trainees will spend hours practicing before they become full-fledged FBI agents.

is no casual matter. It takes a special caliber of professional to earn acceptance to the FBI Academy and successfully complete the training. If you make it into the ranks of agents, you can expect unpredictable schedules, long hours, and periodic transfers.

The basic requirements are simple enough: You must be a U.S. citizen between the ages of 23 and 37, with a bachelor's degree from an accredited college. Generally, applicants are also required to have a record of three years' satisfactory, full-time employment. Sometimes, individuals with certain special training and skills are considered without the employment history. Law school and accounting graduates, for example, have already been taught much about the law and legal rights—essential knowledge for law enforcement officers. Persons who can speak certain foreign languages, meanwhile, may be immensely useful to the bureau for special assignments, regardless of past work experience. You also need a valid driver's license. And your eyesight must be (or be correctable to) at least 20/20 in one eye and 20/40 in the other.

Those credentials will suffice to get your application read and placed on file. To receive serious consideration as an FBI agent, however, you must be exceptional in many ways. Acceptance into bureau service is based on stringent testing and background investigation.

Reference checks go far beyond contacting former employers and character witnesses. The bureau talks to your friends, neighbors, and colleagues. Agents fully review your educational, financial, medical, and military records, as well as any police records. You must undergo drug testing and a polygraph ("lie detector") session. Among other topics, agents will quiz you on illicit drug use. (Have you used or sold marijuana during the last three years? If so, your aspirations of joining the FBI must be placed on hold.) The research is so thorough it can take up to four months for the bureau's human resource personnel to complete their hiring investigations.

New recruits must undergo more than 600 hours of stringent training in 15 weeks at the FBI Academy in Quantico, Virginia (this area is also home, not coincidentally, to a U.S. Marine Corps base). Naturally, they're taught modern methods of crime detection, evidence gathering, and case investigation. They learn to interview witnesses and gain the confidence of informants. They study behavioral science (psychology) and master certain computer programs.

Law courses at the academy drill potential agents in the dos and don'ts of criminal procedures such as search and seizure and suspects' detention rights. They learn the legal fine points of what constitutes "probable cause" in making an arrest.

Trainees learn to recognize and use a variety of firearms; they must become good enough on the pistol range to hit a target 50 yards away—with either hand! They're also instructed in self-defense techniques. Physical exercise regimens during this period are grueling.

Near the end of their training, students are introduced to "Hogan's Alley." This simulated urban street scene, created in 1987, presents actors in crime simulations that require the trainees to make quick decisions and use the different skills they've learned.

Once you graduate from the academy and receive your first assignment, training is not over. Agents are occasionally ordered to return to Quantico for special short courses.

Agents must go wherever they are needed. They should expect to be transferred frequently during their first decade or longer. Only after 10 years of service in one office may they be taken off "nonvoluntary rotation" and offered "voluntary rotation."

The term "burn out" is well known among FBI agents. Regular involvement with callous people and savage acts does not leave an agent unscarred. Before pursuing a career with the bureau, interested persons should learn all they can about the life of an agent.

Not everyone who works with—or for—the FBI is an agent. From the beginning, the FBI has used civilian workers to assist field detectives. In one early example, the investigation of the kidnapping of aviator Charles Lindbergh's infant son, law enforcement agencies engaged:

♦ An artist to sketch the face of the prime suspect;
♦ Bank officials and private businessmen and women to help trace the ransom money after it was spent (a report from a New York gas station attendant more than two years after the crime proved crucial in the ultimate arrest);
♦ A U.S. forestry official who was an expert in wood varieties and carpentry tools to glean every possible clue from the wooden ladder apparently used by the kidnapper;
♦ Phonograph engineers to record the voice of the go-between who delivered the ransom money, who reconstructed the conversations he'd had with the

kidnapping operative, imitating the criminal's vocal inflections and diction.

Today, the FBI also employs support personnel, such as clerical staff, language specialists, lab technicians, electricians and electronics technicians, legal professionals, administrative professionals, computer programmers, and carpenters. Naturally, requirements for these support workers are not as demanding as for agents, and they do not undergo the rigorous training program at Quantico. But they must have excellent records. Educational requirements range from high school diplomas to technical college diplomas to university master's degrees, depending on the job roles. Each candidate's primary asset, in the eyes of the bureau, is his or her specialized knowledge or skill.

For more information about FBI work and career opportunities, visit the bureau's website at www.fbi.gov. No matter what role you might be interested in and qualified to play—agent, civilian expert, or support staff—the FBI could certainly provide an opportunity for an interesting and exciting career.

CRIME LAB:
A SCIENTIFIC APPROACH TO CRIME FIGHTING

An FBI agent marks points on a fingerprint found at a crime scene, so that it can be compared to others in the Bureau's national fingerprint database. Since the 19th century, fingerprinting has been recognized as one of the most reliable methods of identifying criminals.

Criminals have become increasingly sophisticated in plotting and carrying out many different kinds of misdeeds. To deal with them, law enforcement agencies have likewise become sophisticated. In fact, the modern approach to criminal investigation is scientific, to a great extent. "Forensic science"—meaning applying science to legal problems—is now a vital weapon in the war against crime. A state-of-the-art crime lab resembles a science laboratory in many ways, complete with chemicals, test tubes, and microscopes.

Early initiatives in using math and science to help solve crimes date to the late Victorian era. This was the period when a fictitious detective named Sherlock Holmes with his "scientific methods" was becoming the rage in English popular literature. In 1873, a statistician named Alphonse Bertillon in Paris convinced police to make records of convicts' precise physical measurements. Bertillon knew such features as the dimensions of the skull and the length of the limbs remain constant after a person becomes an adult.

This system of taking and filing measurements to help identify criminal suspects was never widely used. It was soon replaced worldwide by a simpler, more reliable method of criminal identification: fingerprinting.

It was the English anthropologist Sir Francis Galton who determined that no two people have the same fingerprints. Fingerprinting began to be used by police agencies in the 1880s. Within a decade, police in England and Argentina were establishing the first official systems of classifying prints.

In 1893, an Austrian judge named Hans Gross wrote a book advocating "criminalistics," the systematic gathering and analysis of evidence in criminal investigations. Gross regarded proper evidence handling as a science. The idea was developed further by a French doctor, Edmond Locard, who set up one of the first known crime laboratories in 1910.

In America, the first crime lab is believed to have been established by Los Angeles officials in 1923. Some 250 crime labs are used by American law enforcement agencies today. The most sophisticated is the facility created and refined by the FBI.

The FBI's Technical Laboratory was created in 1932. There, professionals started conducting criminal investigations in much the same way scientists performed experiments, using microscopes, chemicals, and other aids. They began amassing special collections that would be helpful in tracing villains and contraband (stolen goods). To the bureau's fingerprint collection, which had already been started, were added samples of tire treads (to help trace and identify vehicles used in criminal acts), typefaces (to help categorize typewritten communications), watermarks engrained in paper, and, naturally, a broad variety of guns.

Operating outside the media spotlight, the FBI lab quietly began proving its worth in resolving countless mysteries. Often, cases were made when small pieces of evidence were identified and connected to a suspect—evidence that would have been overlooked by prior generations of investigators.

A major early case that took advantage of the lab's forensic powers was the 1955 explosion of an airplane in Colorado. Large and miniscule fragments of the aircraft, luggage, and personal belongings of the victims were studied at the laboratory. Examiners concluded a bomb had been planted among the cargo. Working with state authorities, the FBI ultimately zeroed in on the bomber, who confessed and was convicted.

Today, the FBI's crime lab has more than 600 workers. They examine and analyze evidence in thousands of cases annually—not just for the bureau, but for law enforcement agencies across the country that don't have lab facilities or forensic specialists of their own. The lab makes an estimated two million fingerprint examinations every year.

The bureau's Civil Identification Section has more than 170 million sets of fingerprints on record—more than any other country in the world. Its records are used by more than 60,000 U.S. and foreign law enforcement agencies.

There are different methods of finding and lifting fingerprints. Much depends on the type of surface being examined (painted areas, paper, plastic, bare metal) and other circumstances. With print detection advances of recent years, investigators have been able to reexamine physical evidence from cases that went unsolved for decades. Fingerprinting has long been the most obvious form of crime-fighting science. But there are other ways to physically link a suspect, victim, or witness to a crime scene. For example, criminals and others important to an investigation often leave tracks on the ground or floor. In some cases, these forms of evidence have led to the capture of a guilty party.

Wilderness trackers in frontier times learned to

The Federal Bureau of Investigation's forensic experts are skilled in reading the smallest clues. Here, an expert compares plaster casts of shoeprints with an actual shoe. If the shoe fits—if this agent determines the shoe probably made the print from which the plaster cast was made—the shoe's owner may be a suspect.

recognize animal paw tracks and the imprints left by moccasins, boots, and other kinds of footwear. A skilled tracker could determine the approximate height and weight of the beast or human and the age of the tracks.

Modern forensic investigators can do more. Using plaster of Paris, they can make a cast of a suspicious footprint or tire track at or near a crime scene. In numerous instances, successful matches of casts have linked a certain individual or vehicle to a crime and helped secure a conviction.

In one way or another, paper plays a role in almost every crime. In addition to "paper crimes"—fraud, forgery, document theft, common forms of extortion—criminals of all types leave evidence on paper.

Some of these clues consist of the paper itself (a matchbook, receipt or billing statement, cardboard box, parcel or gift wrapping paper, coffee or cold drink cup).

Other clues are found in what's imprinted on the paper. Handwriting analysis can help prove the identity of a person who wrote an incriminating note or letter, or the authenticity of a signed document. Even typewritten and computer-generated messages can be traced to a certain type of machine and sometimes to a specific machine.

Handwriting analysis is called graphology. By examining certain patterns and details of penmanship, experts can tell with a high level of certainty whether two or more writing samples were the work of the same individual.

This kind of evidence was used in the high-profile investigation of the Lindbergh kidnapping shortly after the Bureau of Investigation established its criminal laboratory in 1932. Several years after the crime, authorities placed a suspect named Bruno Richard Hauptmann on trial for kidnapping and murdering the Lindbergh baby. Forensic investigator Charles Appel testified that after extensive handwriting comparisons, he considered it "inconceivable" that the ransom note used in the crime could have been written by anyone but the defendant. This evidence helped convict Hauptmann, who was executed in 1936.

Another highly specialized area of criminal investigation is the study of "ballistics." This is the science of projectiles—most commonly, bullets—in motion.

By closely examining spent bullets and suspect weapons, experts can determine whether a certain gun fired a certain bullet. That's because the interior of every gun barrel has a unique "fingerprint," a set of minute imperfections in the metal that make marks on a bullet as it's fired. In this way, ballistics testing can be as valuable to crime solving as fingerprint matching.

Like fingerprints and bullets, countless other items can connect a suspect to a crime scene and bring about successful prosecution. When leaving the scene of a crime, criminals may inadvertently leave behind a single hair, a tiny fiber of clothing, a bit of soil from the

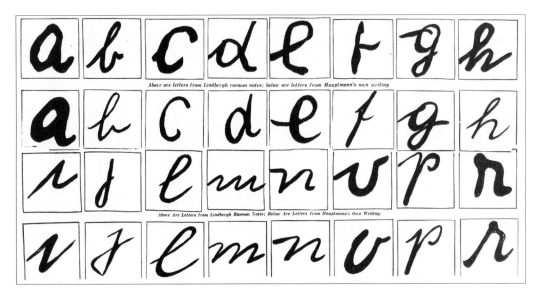

Above are letters from Lindbergh ransom notes; below are letters from Hauptmann's own writing

Above Are Letters from Lindbergh Ransom Notes; Below Are Letters from Hauptmann's Own Writing.

Graphology, the study of handwriting, is a useful technique in identifying criminals. In the infamous Lindbergh kidnapping of the 1930s, a forensic investigator helped convict Bruno Hauptmann by comparing a sample of his writing (second and fourth lines) with the ransom notes (first and third lines) that Lindbergh received.

sole of their shoe—any of which can eventually bring investigators to their door. Tiny fragments of glass, splinters of wood, or miniscule paint chips found in a suspect's clothing or car can be examined in the crime lab. If these "trace elements" can be shown to come from the crime scene, the investigators' case may be strengthened enormously.

Criminal investigators also employ chemistry in their arsenal of scientific weapons. Acid, for example, can be used to make an obliterated serial number readable again on stolen goods. Certain chemicals are used in analyzing blood and other pieces of evidence. Some high-tech tools in a crime lab might include:

- ◆ A gas chromatograph, which can separate the parts of a substance (useful in determining the percentage of alcohol or other drugs in the bloodstream);
- ◆ A spectrophotometer, which can sense invisible light and heat rays (useful in examining, for example, the characteristics of ink on paper);
- ◆ X-ray machines.

A form of forensic science being used more frequently in recent years is DNA testing and profiling, or

"DNA fingerprinting." DNA (deoxyribonucleic acid) is found in human cells. Scientists consider it extremely unlikely that any two individuals have the same DNA pattern.

In past generations, if a criminal left a drop of blood or a hair at a crime scene investigators could use the blood type or hair color to help narrow the field of suspects. Today, thanks to DNA profiling, those small bits of evidence can arguably lead not just to a class of people who have the same blood type or hair color, but to a specific individual. At the same time, DNA testing can help prove the innocence of wrongly arrested suspects. DNA can also be taken from bone fragments and semen. This places those additional substances at the disposal of modern-day investigators.

DNA science is not 100 percent exact. Defense attorneys often challenge DNA reports, sometimes successfully. They also challenge other forms of FBI crime lab results—again, sometimes with success. And sometimes the FBI gives them good reason to try: The crime lab came under scrutiny in the late 1990s when a lab scientist accused employees in certain sections of misconduct and questionable practices. After an 18-month probe, the Department of Justice's inspector general concluded that most of the charges were not substantiated, but "some important ones were." He noted that some laboratory examiners had given testimony that was flawed or beyond their expertise in several cases, including the World Trade Center bombing. In other cases, such as the Oklahoma City bombing, examiners filed incorrect or incomplete reports. The inspector general recommended that the lab's Explosives Unit be restructured and that improvements be made in management and case documentation.

Despite criticisms, the FBI's crime lab remains the world's foremost forensic resource. No method—or organization—is perfect, but the FBI strives to provide the most accurate forensic data possible.

MENTAL
PURSUIT

For 17 years, FBI agents failed to find the terrorist known as the Unabomber. It was not until the FBI's psychological profile was publicized in 1995 that Ted Kaczynski was finally apprehended.

In 1995 the FBI publicized a psychological profile of the mysterious fugitive whose nickname was inspiring terror across America: the Unabomber. For 17 years agents had been investigating a series of similar bombings—as many as 16—attributed to an individual described as a white male who lived the life of a hermit and was skilled at fashioning things with ordinary hardware store materials. They believed he was from Chicago, where the first bomb had exploded, but now lived in the West. Although antisocial, profilers reasoned, the suspect was hardly likely to strike acquaintances as the type of person who would kill and maim. When he was ultimately caught, they predicted, police would find him well-educated, well-organized, and amiable, the kind of person who makes "an ideal neighbor."

To David Kaczynski, a social worker in Schenectady, New York, it seemed the FBI was describing his older brother Theodore. A Chicago native and Harvard graduate at age 20, Theodore "Ted" Kaczynski,

When David Kaczynski read the FBI profile of the Unabomber, he believed the terrorist might be his estranged brother.

now in his fifties, had abandoned a career as a math professor in California and moved to the Montana mountains. He had become a hermit indeed, living in a primitive shack and growing what he ate—which he shared with a neighbor. He got around on a bicycle he had constructed from assorted pieces.

It was a tip from David Kaczynski the following year that focused the FBI manhunt on Theodore's Montana wilderness home and ultimately led to the arrest of the Unabomber.

By that time criminal profiling had become an important, commonly used tool, especially in solving serial crimes. For example, an FBI profiler had helped police zero in on the ghastly Trailside Killer of San Francisco Bay in the early 1980s. A number of hikers, mostly women, had been shot or stabbed to death in and around Mount Tamalpais Park. The profile suggested a white man with a record of attempted rape. He was intelligent but had psychological problems dating to childhood, the early symptoms of which may have included bed-wetting and animal abuse. Remarkably, the profile even predicted that the killer had a speech defect.

The man police ultimately arrested had a sex crime record and was the product of a troubled childhood involving abuse by his parents, animal cruelty, bed-wetting, and ridicule because he stuttered.

This kind of "mental pursuit" is another way modern detectives track fugitives. They learn everything they can about the person's way of thinking. Psychological specialists study the circumstances and evidence of a crime and try to compose a detailed, accurate "profile" of the criminal.

Typically, this technique is used to help identify and predict the future actions of "UNSUBs"—unidentified subjects. It is especially productive in serial cases, where similar crimes are repeated by the same person over a period of time.

Profiling has evolved since the early 1980s as a highly effective tool for criminal investigation. It is not mere guesswork. Often, by the time a suspect is caught, the profiler on the case can reveal things about the person that were unknown to the suspect's own close relatives and friends.

The FBI's first official criminal profiler was John Douglas. Douglas, who retired in 1995, was assigned to the FBI Academy's Behavioral Science Division in Quantico, Virginia. He began learning his specialty by studying past serial crimes and interviewing the convicted perpetrators in prison. He has written several chilling books describing his "journeys" into the minds of killers.

Profilers aren't usually in the line of fire every day, like certain other types of agents. But their task is so stressful it often causes work-related illnesses ranging from ulcers to depression to chest pains and neurological disorders. Nevertheless, they are proving to be vital in identifying, apprehending, and prosecuting offenders who are particularly dangerous—"the worst of the worst," profiler Jim Wright says.

Kidnapping, for example, is among the types of crime that may warrant calling on the profiler's special knowledge. Kidnapping is the ultimate form of extortion. Most victims taken for ransom are not released. Why not? Because usually the victims are abducted by people they know and trust. The kidnappers feel compelled to dispose of these condemning "witnesses."

The expertise of profilers is increasingly in demand. Federal profilers are constantly called in to advise municipal, county, and state law enforcement agencies. On occasion, Douglas has worked on more than 150 cases at a time.

Human behavior is the profiler's stock-in-trade. Unhappily, Douglas points out, human behavior "is not an exact science." And it is extremely complicated. "To do what we do," he writes, "it's very important to get into the mind of not only the killer or the UNSUB, but into the mind of the victim at the time the crime occurred. That's the only way you're going to be able to understand the dynamics of the crime—what was going on between the victim and the offender."

It's certainly *not* pleasant work. Envisioning what it must have been like for the victim of a murder, rape, or other brutal crime, Douglas explains, is "among the most devastating emotional exercises imaginable." The criminals who draw the attention of profilers often are not robbers or embezzlers who seek material gain, but deviants who "kill or rape or torture because they enjoy it, because it gives them satisfaction and a feeling of domination and control so lacking from every other aspect of their shabby, inadequate, and cowardly lives."

Every crime has a motive, investigators know. (That's one thing that distinguishes it from an "accident.") In his book *Journey Into Darkness*, Douglas writes: "When you've analyzed what should be the motive based on the crime scenario and that doesn't make sense, and you go through all the other 'logical' ones and you can't make one of them fit reasonably, then you start looking into psychiatric territory."

To the greatest extent possible, profilers intentionally distance themselves from the day-to-day investigation of a crime. They don't want to know the identities or characteristics of actual suspects at any given time because they have to be completely objective and unbiased. It's a strange role.

Douglas says whenever he was asked to profile an unknown criminal, "the one thing I did not want from the investigators was any information on suspects they might have developed. I wanted to remain objective, my profile based solely on what the evidence suggested to me."

Jud Ray, another former FBI profiler, calls this the profiler's "freedom of neutrality." Ray was the first FBI profiler to testify in a court trial. Until that 1987 case, involving the grotesque rape/murder of an Alaska woman and her two small daughters, profiling was not accepted by courts as proven "expert witness" testimony.

Profilers are useful not only in identifying criminals but in helping demonstrate the innocence of other suspects. For example, FBI behavioral experts spent much time and effort helping local police agencies solve a series of related burglaries, rapes, and murders in Virginia during the mid-1980s. The result was the conviction and execution of a man clearly proven to be the criminal—and the release of another who had been wrongly imprisoned after plea bargaining in one of the crimes.

Popular movies and TV shows have interested many young people in the profiler's profession. It appears to be an intriguing, exciting, and greatly challenging career in which you can do much good on behalf of society. Enthusiasts may not realize how stressful the work is and how difficult it is for a profiler to "leave the job at the office."

Nor do they realize how hard it is to become a member of the FBI's profiling unit. Profilers are selected not from the psychiatric profession or the world of academics, but from within the bureau's own ranks of trained, experienced, and exceptionally creative field agents. The profiling unit's recruits, already proven in criminal investigations, undergo two years of tough, intensive training in the profiler's field. Part of their training includes actual case studies, working alongside experienced profilers to learn from them.

Unknowing observers believe the profiler's profession basically boils down to mathematics. Study the evidence, the precise history of the case, the similarities between victims and geographic locations, the villain's obvious *modus operandi* (standard way of operating) . . . then punch all the factors into a computer and watch a perfect description of the culprit—the mathematical "solution"—print out. This is not so. Each case is different. Patterns of thought and action can be pieced together, but small distinctions arise. The profiler must be able to use judgment and instinct, based on years of experience, to be able to discard certain formulas that almost—but not quite—pinpoint a suspect.

Jud Ray says the profiler's special abilities are "a collection of all the disciplines and an understanding and a good depth of knowledge about forensic psychology, forensic pathology, cultural anthropology, social psychology, motivational psychology—all of the things that when they are properly aligned and understood with a sense of investigative technique behind you, you have all these things kind of synchronized."

"No one in my unit ever claims to be able to deliver up the name and identity of a particular UNSUB," writes Douglas. "All we can do is describe the type of individual we think did it based on the information we're given and what kind of pre- and post-offense behavior we would expect to see. In that way, we hope to be able to help investigators narrow down their list of suspects."

It works. In a growing number of cases, it's the profiler's assessment that makes a complicated case suddenly come together for the investigative team. Arrest and conviction often quickly follow.

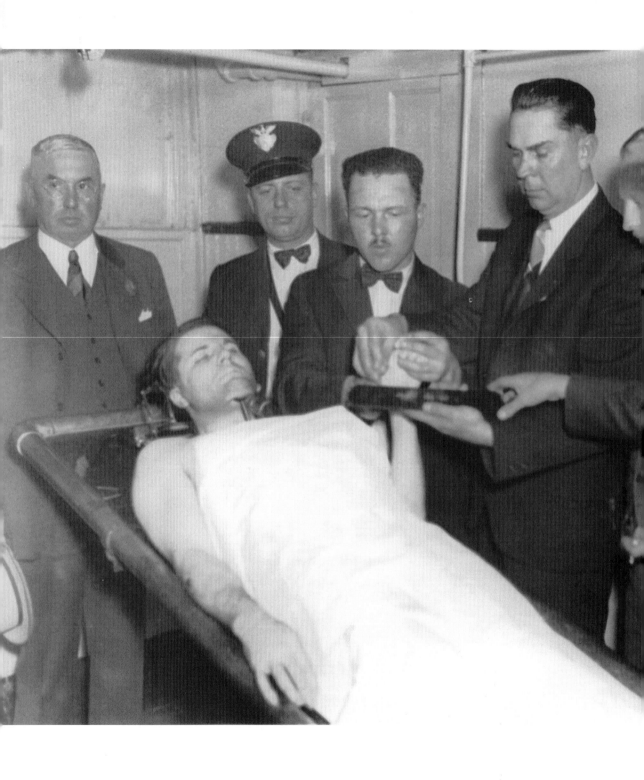

FAMOUS CASES

The Bureau of Investigation was introduced to America in the sensational news coverage of the gangster era. Even today, many of its most famous cases are those involving the notorious bank robbers and mobsters of the 1930s. Of course, that era was only the beginning of the FBI's importance in the pursuit of America's criminals. Numerous later cases also caused sensations and kept the FBI's crime-fighting efforts in the headlines.

Let's take a look through the FBI's gallery of well-known cases.

Charles Arthur Floyd, better known as "Pretty Boy Floyd," died in a gun battle with federal agents in 1934. Many believed Floyd was earlier involved in the "Kansas City Massacre," a failed attempt to free federal prisoner Frank Nash from the hands of the police. Five men, including Nash, died in the showdown.

PRETTY BOY FLOYD

He always denied involvement (and some historians agree), but Charles Arthur "Pretty Boy" Floyd is still best known as one of three gunman in the "Kansas City Massacre" of June 1933.

Bureau of Investigation agents and police officers were transporting a federal prisoner, Frank Nash, when several of Nash's underworld associates ambushed them in the parking area of the Kansas City, Missouri, train station. Three policemen, one federal agent, and the prisoner were all killed by machine gun fire. Investigators identified the killers as 37-year-old Vernon C. Miller, the leader; 23-year-old Adam C. Richetti; and 29-year-old Floyd.

Floyd and Richetti, both fugitives at the time, had been traveling together for several months, committing holdups and stealing cars—constantly running from the law. After temporarily taking a Missouri sheriff captive, they reportedly arrived in Kansas City the night before the famous shooting. They took refuge with Miller, a one-time South Dakota lawman who had joined the midwestern gangster realm. Miller had been assigned by underworld leaders to carry out the Nash "rescue" mission. Floyd and Richetti apparently agreed to join him. The three were waiting, concealed among parked cars, when Nash and the officers emerged from the Union Railway Station shortly after 7 A.M. on June 17.

The shooting was over within 30 seconds. The law officers barely had time to draw their guns; those who survived instinctively jumped for cover. Realizing they'd accidentally shot Nash, the attackers immediately fled.

Regardless of whether Floyd was one of the Kansas City ambushers, he was unquestionably a major criminal. A poor Oklahoma farm boy, he grew up tall, handsome, and muscular. He married, settled on a farm, and, by most accounts, was eager to earn a living. But farms were failing and there was little work. Embittered and desperate, Floyd robbed a company payroll shipment in St. Louis, Missouri, at age 24. Arrested a few weeks later, he served three years in prison.

After his release, Floyd began an irreversible life outside the law. Almost immediately, he was suspected in the disappearance and probable murder of a man he believed had killed his father but had been acquitted of wrongdoing. Determined never to be imprisoned again, Floyd went to Kansas City to avoid questioning. There he joined the underworld. It was 1929—the year the stock market crash plunged the nation into the Great Depression.

Floyd joined a gang that began holding up a string of small-town Ohio banks. In one getaway, the robbers killed a pursuing highway patrolman, then crashed into a telephone pole. They were caught, tried, and convicted—but Floyd escaped by diving out the window of a train while being taken to prison.

With a new partner, he began holding up banks first in Michigan, then Kentucky. The spree ended with a shootout that left his partner, a girlfriend, and a policeman dead and Floyd fleeing for his life. He eventually returned to Kansas City and was able to live in hiding for several months. Inevitably, though, government agents learned of his whereabouts. After another shoot-out, Floyd escaped again, leaving another detective dead.

This time, Floyd returned to his homeland, the hills of Oklahoma, for protection. He had many friends there. They admired him as a Robin Hood figure because he stole from the rich (banks) and, it was said, gave money to poor farmers so they could avoid foreclosure. He and an accomplice spent the next two years robbing Oklahoma banks and avoiding the law. They reputedly robbed two banks in a single day. Their frequent raids caused insurance rates in the state to skyrocket.

During the four years leading up to the Kansas City Massacre, Floyd committed countless bank robberies in some half dozen states. Along the way, he killed or was involved in the killing of at least three law enforcement officers and two citizens (not including his father's alleged slayer). Investigators believe he may have killed as many as 10 people.

After the "Massacre," Floyd and Richetti made their way to Buffalo, New York, where they rented an apartment with their common-law wives. A year later, the two couples were returning by car to Oklahoma when an accident forced them to stop for repairs in Wellsville, Ohio. The town's suspicious police chief, J. H. Fulz, arrested Richetti after a gun battle that sent Floyd running through the countryside.

Melvin Purvis, the Bureau of Investigation's Chicago chief, led a dragnet (a manhunt) by federal and local officers to locate the fugitive. They closed in on him at an Ohio farm. He was shot as he ran across a field, wielding a pistol. As he lay dying, he uttered a final denial of participation in the Kansas City train station attack.

Richetti was convicted and sent to the gas chamber in Missouri four years later. Miller, the apparent leader of the Kansas City gunmen, had been killed in Detroit, Michigan, about six months after the "Massacre"— apparently by a rival gangster.

AL CAPONE

Probably the best-known gangster of the 1920s and 1930s was Al "Scarface" Capone. The Capone gang in Chicago—a virtual army of criminals numbering in the hundreds—carried out appalling atrocities against rival underworld groups and individuals. Hapless citizens as well as police were victims during Capone's reign of terror. It's been estimated more than 1,000 people died as a result of Capone gang activities.

Capone avoided directly incriminating himself in the bloodbaths he ordered. When U.S. Treasury Department and FBI agents did manage to bring him to

Al "Scarface" Capone was the most notorious gangster of the 1920s and 1930s. Capone eluded the FBI for years until it teamed up with the Treasury Department to pin him down with a conviction for tax evasion.

justice, it was for nonviolent infractions like tax evasion and contempt of court.

Born in New York in 1899, Capone was a school dropout who joined a Brooklyn gang as a teenager. By 1920 he was involved in organized crime in Chicago, and in 1925 he became the leader of one of Chicago's most powerful racketeering operations. By bribing reporters, police officials, and judges, Capone carried on gambling, booze distribution, and other illegal activities practically immune to punishment.

Gangland warfare's goriest moment occurred on Valentine's Day 1929. Seven men associated with Capone's main rival, "Bugs" Moran, were lured into a Chicago garage and mowed down with machine guns by mobsters dressed as policemen. Although Capone's involvement was never provable in court—and he was in Florida at the time of the "St. Valentine's Day Massacre"—most crime historians believe the killers were Capone henchmen.

The "Massacre" provoked public horror and government determination to stop Capone. Three months after the mass execution, he was arrested for carrying a concealed weapon. He quietly served a nine-month sentence, continuing to run his organization from behind bars.

Judgment day came in October 1931. Taken to court on charges of tax evasion and Prohibition violations, Capone apparently tried to buy his way off the hook but failed. He was convicted by a jury and lost on appeals, and he was sentenced to 11 years and heavy fines. He was released from prison in November 1939 after serving seven and a half years.

Capone didn't return to society as an underworld czar. Venereal disease had rendered him mentally incompetent during his incarceration. He died in seclusion in 1947 at his lavish Florida estate.

THE NAZI SABOTEURS

For most of us today, tales of World War II, while fascinating, hold no particular terror. That's because we know how the war ended—good triumphed over Hitler's evil. Americans faced many horrible ordeals and lost many battles, but in time the aggressors were put down and our freedom was preserved.

But to Americans who lived during the war years (1941–45), life was uncertain and unnerving. The Axis powers possessed a brutally effective war machine, and they threatened America from both the Atlantic and Pacific Oceans. While hundreds of thousands of our soldiers, sailors, and pilots fought in Europe and the Pacific islands, their loved ones back home—particularly along the east and west coasts—lived under the constant fear of invasion. "Blackouts" (mandatory curfews and lighting bans) were in force along the shorelines, lest the lights help enemy invaders get their bearings at night while approaching from sea.

America was never invaded on a catastrophic scale, but Germany did manage to land spies and saboteurs on our coasts. During the war, the FBI was America's agency designated to thwart foreign subversives. In June 1942, agents apprehended two teams of German saboteurs who landed in New York and Florida.

Arriving off the coast by submarine, four Germans carrying massive explosives beached on Long Island and another four landed near Jacksonville. They intended to plant bombs in eastern factories that produced war materials for the Allied effort. In the process, they would terrorize Americans on the home front and hopefully weaken our resolve to stay in the war.

These men—all of whom had lived in the United States before the war and spoke English—were trained intensively in explosives, mechanics, electronics, and chemistry, as well as special military tactics. They were taught exactly where to plant bombs in factories, along waterways, and aboard trains for the most devastating effect.

Interestingly, the saboteurs wore German uniforms when they arrived. Why? Because if they were caught, they wanted to be treated not as plainclothes spies (who would quickly be executed) but as military prisoners of war (who would be imprisoned, with the hope of being exchanged or eventually released). Once they got ashore without incident, they buried their military clothes and dressed as civilians.

In times of war, the FBI has intervened to prevent sabotage attempts, as in 1942 when Herbert Hans Haupt (above) and seven other men landed on the Atlantic coast of the United States, armed with large amounts of explosives intended to damage factories making war matériel. Fortunately, the FBI apprehended the eight saboteurs before they could execute any of their plans.

The New York group made their way into New York City the day after arriving. But they had been seen by a Coast Guard patrolman, and their leader feared the American authorities were already on their trail. Not wanting to be captured and prosecuted as a spy, he contacted the FBI and provided information that led to the arrest of all the Germans. Within two weeks of landing, both landing groups had been caught. Though they brought ashore a frightening quantity of explosives, they were unable to carry out a single act of terrorism.

Six of the eight commandos were executed. The other two were jailed and, after the war, released.

THE BRINK'S ROBBERY

When stories of cops and robbers are told, the "Brink's job" of 1950 is frequently among them. The famous security company heist is still considered by some to have been the "crime of the century" because of its brilliant planning and near-perfect execution.

Early one January evening, a band of robbers wearing Halloween masks, chauffeur's caps, and dark blue heavy-weather coats walked through a playground, broached several locked doors in the block-long Brink's North Terminal Garage in Boston, Massachusetts, and accosted the night staff at gunpoint. Brink's was a security company; money and valuables from business customers were stored and sorted at the terminal before being shipped out in armored cars. The gunmen tied the hands of the employees and taped their mouths. Then they dragged away heavy bags containing the day's assets: almost $3 million in cash, checks, money orders, and securities. More than $1.2 million of it was in bills. The robbery took less than 20 minutes.

The investigation took much, much longer. Police and FBI agents immediately began questioning underworld operatives in Boston and other cities.

The Brink's job was the brainchild of a man named

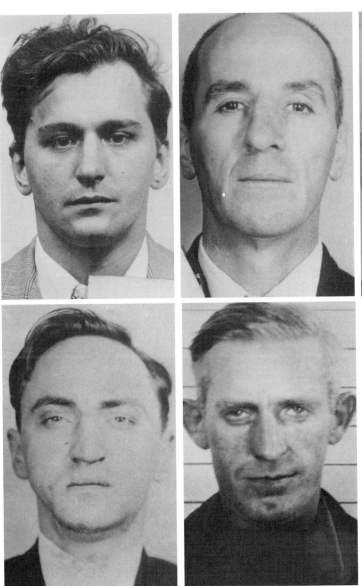

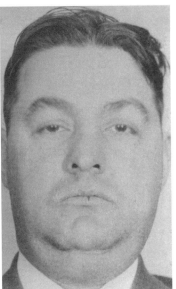

Many historians have called the Brink's bank robbery the "crime of the century." It took the FBI 6 long years to track down the team of 11 felons (5 of whom are pictured above), who in the 1950 robbery ran away with almost $3 million.

Anthony Pino. He engaged 10 fellow crime professionals to help pull off the robbery. They observed the Brink's building for a year and a half. They learned how the burglar alarm system worked, memorized the layout, and removed and reinstalled door locks in order to make their own set of keys. Astonishingly, they even took practice runs of the robbery inside the building to determine anything that could possibly go wrong. As a result, when the time came, nothing went wrong. They knew the Brink's building and the money-handling procedures practically as well as the guards did.

Brink's posted a $100,000 reward, and hundreds of tips were given to police. Almost all were found to be worthless. But agents did find the remains of a truck believed to have been used by the robbers. The vehicle had been cut into pieces with a blowtorch; the pieces were left in bags at a trash dump in nearby Stoughton, Massachusetts.

Investigators eventually deduced the identities of most of the men involved. Two of the key suspects lived in the Stoughton area, where the dismantled truck was found. Another suspect, identified early in the investigation, was Pino.

Pino was known in the Boston underworld as a thorough planner—the kind of criminal capable of organizing the Brink's job. But Pino had a strong alibi: he had been at a neighborhood liquor store at approximately the time of the crime, talking to the store owner and a policeman. The policeman confirmed Pino's story.

Agents weren't convinced. The liquor store wasn't far from the Brink's building, and Pino could have been at both places within a short time. (It was later established that Pino wasn't with the gang who actually entered the Brink's building; he was waiting in the getaway truck on a back street.) But proving it would be difficult. And overall, evidence was thin against all the suspects.

The break came when one of the robbers, Joseph "Specs" O'Keefe, turned informant. O'Keefe was sent to prison soon after the Brink's robbery, convicted of an unrelated burglary. While serving his time, he became angry at some of his cronies because he believed they were cheating him out of much of his share of the Brink's loot. After being released, his bitterness toward the other gang members intensified.

For four years, the crime officially remained unsolved, but Pino and the others worried about O'Keefe's loyalty. On three occasions, he was almost killed by other underworld figures. In one terrifying machine gun attack on the streets of Manchester, Massachusetts, O'Keefe was critically wounded but managed to escape. Elmer "Trigger" Burke, a top hit man for Boston-area criminal rings, was ultimately arrested for that assassination attempt—and by then O'Keefe was back in prison on another unrelated conviction.

For another year, O'Keefe stewed behind bars, furious at the other robbers. Realizing he likely would spend most of his remaining life in jail while his partners lived high on the Brink's treasure, he finally decided to give FBI agents a full account. It was January 1956—six years after the famous robbery.

Six of the 11 gang members were immediately arrested based on O'Keefe's testimony. O'Keefe and one other robber were already in jail, and another was dead. The two remaining criminals dodged arrest until May 1956, when they were surprised by law enforcement officers raiding a Dorchester, Massachusetts, apartment. Tried and convicted of robbery, the Brink's bandits received life sentences.

RUSSIAN SPIES

International espionage is usually perceived as a matter for the Central Intelligence Agency. Frequently, however, the FBI is also involved.

One famous case during the 1950s was the capture and conviction of Rudolf Ivanovich Abel. Abel was a Russian spy who entered the United States illegally from Canada during the late 1940s or early 1950s. He set up a false identity in New York City, where he maintained a surreptitious photography and short-wave radio operation. Abel produced many coded messages

In 1953 the FBI helped apprehend the Russian spy Rudolf Ivanovich Abel, who stored his secret information in hollowed-out jewelry and coins. A hollow nickel that Abel accidentally passed to a newsboy led to his capture.

on tiny pieces of paper that could be concealed and carried by his network of agents in hollowed-out jewelry, coins, shaving utensils, and other ordinary items.

It was the accidental interception of one of these small containers that led to his eventual unmasking. In June 1953, a newsboy was handed a strange-feeling nickel as change while making his collection rounds. When he dropped it, the nickel broke apart. Inside he found a miniscule photograph of a seemingly meaningless set of numbers.

The coin and microphotograph ended up in the

hands of a New York detective, who in turn gave it to the FBI. Eventually, it was linked to a former Soviet operative who was appealing to the U.S. government for asylum. This agent told bureau investigators about a New York spy contact he'd known as "Mark"—who turned out to be Abel.

In 1957, Abel was convicted on several conspiracy charges and imprisoned. Less than five years later, he was exchanged for an American military pilot who had been shot down on an alleged spy mission over Russia. The Abel investigation came to be known as the "Hollow Nickel Case."

These are only a few of the important cases the FBI has solved during its near-century of existence. The FBI also played the central role in gathering evidence following the Kennedy assassination in 1963, the shootings of Dr. Martin Luther King Jr. and Robert F. Kennedy in 1968, and other attempts on the lives of public figures before and since then. In addition, it has solved hundreds of other less publicized, but no less important, crimes.

THE FBI TODAY

Since the death of J. Edgar Hoover in 1972, the FBI has been headed by a varied succession of directors, some of whom departed amid political controversies after brief terms. The current director, Louis J. Freeh, took office September 1, 1993.

Freeh had been a judge and federal prosecutor, as well as a six-year veteran of the bureau. As a prosecutor working with FBI agents in New York, he was perhaps best known for his successful prosecution of the "Pizza Connection" case, in which 18 members of a heroin ring operating between the United States and Italy were convicted.

When he took office, Freeh announced that he

The 1993 standoff between the government and members of David Koresh's Branch Davidian cult ended in the deaths of 4 ATF agents and 81 cult members; the latter perished when a fire consumed the Branch Davidians' compound. Many suspected that federal agents had started the fatal fire, but an independent investigation in 2000 cleared the FBI of any wrongdoing.

Louis J. Freeh was named director of the FBI in 1993. Before taking this position, Freeh was a prosecutor who had made himself known through his successful prosecution of the heroin ring known as the "Pizza Connection."

wanted to streamline the bureau's organization and administration. He did this by merging certain divisions, transferring hundreds of administrative agents into the field to work as investigators, and shutting down or reorganizing some of the bureau's special offices. He raised the standards of conduct among bureau personnel and appointed minorities to higher positions.

Freeh also took steps to strengthen cooperation between the FBI and other law enforcement agencies both within and outside the United States. Agencies began a more concerted effort to share information, aerial surveillance resources, and technology. He has appeared abroad to encourage foreign citizens to join their police agencies in the universal fight against crime.

In addition to serving as FBI director, Freeh was appointed director of the DOJ's Office of Investigative Agency Policies. In this role, he seeks to develop stronger cooperation among different Department of Justice law enforcement offices.

Most of the crimes of yesterday continue to plague us today. But added to them are a whole new generation of crimes. The nature, composition, and priorities of the Federal Bureau of Investigation are constantly changing to meet new demands.

The popular 1930s image of the FBI—G-men engaging mobsters in ferocious gun battles on city streets—lingers, to an extent. But gone are the days of simplistic "cop and robber" dramas. Agents of the 21st century face criminal elements just as cold-blooded and ruthless as the notorious gangland leaders . . . but far more sophisticated and sinister.

FBI agents still investigate professional mobsters and hit men . . . but now, they also have to contend with youthful but powerful street gangs and networks whose narcotics-based domains and brutal rivalries threaten public safety just as alarmingly as Al Capone's tommy-gunners did in 1930s Chicago. They still track kidnappers whose deeds are as heartrending as the abduction of the Lindbergh infant in 1932, but increasingly they also find themselves haunted and taunted by psychopathic serial abductors who torment and kill their victims as an expression of "power." They still probe counterfeiting and fraud operations . . . but many of today's paper criminals are extremely high-tech, which means the FBI has to be on the cutting edge of technology in order to bring them to justice.

In the early years, bombings of buildings and cars by gangsters and political subversives were not unknown. Today's terrorists are more devious. They might send a bomb through the mail—not always as a suspicious-looking parcel, but sometimes as a thin, ordinary-looking letter. In January 1997, agents retrieved eight holiday cards that had been mailed by terrorists from Egypt to targets in Kansas and Washington, D.C. Opening the cards would have activated explosive devices inside them.

A crime unknown until the second half of the 20th century was skyjacking. The first was carried out in 1961 after three decades of commercial air travel. Piracy on the seas and truck hijackings on land were nothing new, but the notion of *air* piracy was so preposterous it stunned the nation and the world. Yet it became a common occurrence during the 1960s and 1970s, typically carried out by international political extremists. In 1969, no fewer than 40 skyjackings were attempted.

Probably the most intriguing skyjacking case—and the only one never solved—was the work not of a political terrorist but of a lone man desperate for money. Listed as "Dan Cooper" on the passenger roster, he boarded a jetliner in Portland, Oregon, in November 1971 and threatened to blow up the plane with a bomb unless the crew obtained for him $200,000 in cash and several parachutes. As the plane flew at 200 miles an hour 10,000 feet over the northwest's Cascade Mountains, Cooper bailed out with the money. Some of the money was found beside a river nine years later, but Cooper was never seen again . . . which means the case officially remains open. FBI agents in the region still receive occasional tips suggesting where to find Cooper, his remains, or more of the cash.

After airports and airlines implemented stringent security measures, the number of skyjackings decreased dramatically. Terrorists began resorting to a far more deadly and dreaded tactic: planting hard-to-detect bombs inside ordinary-looking airline baggage. Today, one of the first causes we consider when we hear of an airline catastrophe is sabotage.

A much more common source of violent crime is the illegal narcotics trade, which mushroomed into a national crisis in the 1960s. It continues today, involving several federal agencies, including the FBI, in addition to state and local law enforcement entities.

Another growing problem is nonviolent but just as insidious: telemarketing crime. Illegal telemarketers may deliver cheap commodities instead of the valuable bargains they promised—or they may disappear within a few days, taking their victims' money or credit card information with them. Frequently, they contact elderly persons and persuade them to "invest" savings in a fraudulent scheme. In 1993, the FBI began Operation Disconnect to combat illegal telemarketers. During the first two years, some 300 individuals were successfully apprehended and convicted.

A peculiar category of FBI record-keeping is the National Stolen Art File (NSAF). The records, maintained on computer, describe not only works of art but cultural artifacts such as rare manuscripts, certain antiques, and items taken from historic sites or archaeological digs. The FBI maintains text descriptions and, if available, photos and drawings of stolen and recovered objects, as well as records of each case. Only law enforcement officials (not museums or private collectors) are allowed to submit an item for inclusion in the file.

Another FBI special program is Awareness of National Security Issues and Response, or ANSIR. It keeps a highly confidential National Security Threat List describing foreign powers and issues that may threaten our nation's security. ANSIR is linked closely to the work of other programs within the bureau, especially those involving international spies and terrorists.

Some recent, widely publicized crimes investigated by the bureau have included:

- ◆ **The World Trade Center Bombing.** In early February 1993, the towering World Trade Center in New York City was rocked by a bomb. The homemade device had been left in a van parked in the building's underground parking garage. More than a thousand people were injured and six died; half a billion dollars in damage resulted from the blast. Four Islamic terrorists were apprehended and sentenced to 240 years imprisonment each; others were convicted on related charges. Eventually, the plot was connected with Usama Bin Laden, an exiled Saudi Arabian millionaire currently on the FBI's "most wanted" list. He is believed to have funded many terrorist assaults against U.S. facilities and citizens in Africa and the Middle East. The conspirators said the World Trade Center bombing was an act of retaliation against U.S. policies in the Middle East.

- ◆ **Operation Polar Cap.** South American drug cartels (monopolies in illegal drug production and trafficking) during the early 1990s were found to be processing their ill-gotten earnings through bank accounts in the United States and other countries. Managing and distributing illicit funds through apparently legitimate accounts and intermediaries is called money "laundering." The FBI worked with

The FBI has remained active in the ongoing U.S. war on drugs, primarily by apprehending international drug lords. In 1996 the FBI apprehended Juan Garcia Abrego, leader of the Gulf Cartel located in Mexico.

customs and tax investigators to bring dozens of participants to justice and confiscate tens of millions of dollars in illegally generated money and other assets.

◆ **Street Gang Activities.** The growing menace of city gangs, often consisting of teenagers and even preteens, frequently calls for the investigative resources of the FBI. Beyond violent crimes, vandalism, and intimidation, many gangs are involved in dangerous power struggles for control of local drug distribution. One of the largest gang investigations culminated in 1994. Agents broke up an organization in western New York State, obtaining several dozen convictions on violations of RICO laws. RICO stands for "racketeer influence and corrupt organization." These laws, meant to make it easier to prosecute criminal organizations, were originally passed to deal with the mafia.

◆ **Operation Twisted Metal.** Accidental collisions make auto travel in a growing population a risky venture. Motorists in recent years have faced an additional worry, particularly on freeways in and near major metropolises: staged auto accidents. Rings of criminals use several subtle techniques to cause wrecks, exaggerate injury claims, and extract heavy payments from auto insurance companies. Schemers typically use two or more vehicles to "trap" and cleverly restrict the free movement of a target car or truck. They then maneuver the traffic flow into an unavoidable accident that, in the eyes of the law, appears to be the targeted driver's fault. Not only does the menace contribute to rising auto insurance costs, but it frequently results in injuries and even deaths. A recent two-year investigation by police and insurance officials in cooperation with the FBI was called Operation Twisted Metal. It resulted in the arrests of more than a dozen alleged accident conspirators in California. Those arrested included lawyers and chiropractors.

◆ **Medal of Honor Violations.** A 1995 investigation uncovered an illicit military medals scam. Visitors to military collectible shows were able to buy allegedly authentic U.S. Medals of Honor. Federal law forbids the unauthorized manufacture of military awards, as well as their sale or the wearing of them by a nonrecipient. The Medal of Honor, America's highest combat bravery award, was being made under government contract by a New York industrial firm. Agents learned that besides making the contracted medals, the company was also making copies and selling them to a distributor. A number of imposters—many of whom were prominent businessmen and professionals and some of whom had never served in the military—were buying and displaying the medals illegally. The company was prosecuted and barred from further government work.

Other modern-day investigations deal with crimes as diverse as violence at abortion clinics, civil rights infringements, art theft, and—still today, as in the bureau's early years—counterfeiting.

One area that has been receiving more and more attention from the FBI—and criminals—is computer crime. Get-rich-quick schemes and the misuse of corporate finances have been problems in the United States since the early years of independence. But with the increasing popularity of the Internet as a medium for buying and selling in the 1990s, criminals began delving into a new style of monetary crime. Financial officials estimate stock fraud on the Internet—practically unheard of a decade ago—now costs investors a million dollars *per hour* and has become one of the leading types of investment fraud. To help fight the problem, the FBI's Financial Crimes Section, Economic Crimes Unit, has established Operation InvestNet. The bureau is working with the Securities and Exchange Commission, U.S. attorney's offices, and other government entities to look into investment fraud.

Today, investment fraud is only one of many types of crimes that are committed via computers and the Internet. The increasing number and diversity of computer-related crimes has led the FBI to form the National Computer Crime Squad.

The FBI's approach to cyber crime has drawn significant criticism. In response to the growing plague of computer invasions by criminals, some of which have victimized the U.S. military and other government entities, the Justice Department has sought greater high-tech protective and investigative powers. For example, the government made it easier for U.S. corporations to import foreign encryption technology to help protect their computer systems. In July 2000, privacy advocates heavily criticized the FBI's "Carnivore" system. With Carnivore technology, law enforcement officials can "wiretap" electronic mail while investigating criminal suspects online. The issue of whether Carnivore-type methods violate the rights of Internet users is currently under debate.

The FBI is constantly under public scrutiny. Because of this, law enforcement officers at every level are trained to ensure the safety of bystanders and other potential victims while pursuing and fighting criminal suspects. Miscreants often escape after the pursuing officers abort their efforts because of danger to citizens. In certain tragic incidents, though, innocent citizens have been injured and killed in the "pursuit of justice." When that happens, law enforcement officers find themselves under attack from the public they risk their lives to serve.

One of the most widely publicized recent controversies involving the FBI was the 1993 tragedy near Waco, Texas. Members of a religious sect called the Branch Davidians were holed up at their compound for 51 days as federal agents demanded their surrender. Heavily armed, some of the fugitives allegedly killed four ATF officers. The confrontation ended when the compound was suddenly engulfed in flames. Eighty people died in the fire. The government reported that members of the sect ignited the fire themselves; critics contended the fire may have been caused by tear gas launched into the compound. In July 2000, an independent investigation cleared federal agents of responsibility for the fire.

Despite controversies and mistakes, the Federal Bureau of Investigation is one of the most well-respected and effective law enforcement agencies in the world. Its work speaks for itself. In one recent year, the FBI supplied prosecutors with evidence that led to 14,000 criminal convictions. The bureau's ID facilities have led to the location of more than 33,000 fugitives. From airplanes to computer databases to nuclear installations, modern miscreants are finding new places and ways to carry out their dirty work. Wherever they venture, they can expect the FBI to be in close pursuit.

Bibliography

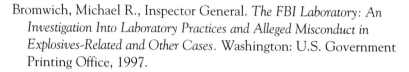

Bromwich, Michael R., Inspector General. *The FBI Laboratory: An Investigation Into Laboratory Practices and Alleged Misconduct in Explosives-Related and Other Cases*. Washington: U.S. Government Printing Office, 1997.

D'Angelo, Laura. *The FBI's Most Wanted*. Philadelphia: Chelsea House, 1997.

Douglas, John, and Mark Olshaker. *Journey Into Darkness*. New York: Scribner, 1997.

———. *Mindhunter: Inside the FBI's Elite Serial Crime Unit*. Thorndike, Maine: G.K. Hall and Co., 1995.

Fisher, David. *Hard Evidence*. New York: Simon and Schuster, 1995.

Gentry, Curt. *J. Edgar Hoover: The Man and His Secrets*. New York: W. W. Norton and Company, 1991.

Gustafson, Anita. *Guilty or Innocent?* New York: Holt, Rinehart and Winston, 1985.

Jeffreys, Diarmuid. *The Bureau: Inside the Modern FBI*. Boston: Houghton Mifflin Company, 1995.

Kerby, Phil. *With Honor and Purpose*. New York: St. Martin's Press, 1998.

Lee, Mary Price, et al. *The 100 Best Careers in Crime Fighting*. New York: Macmillan Reference USA, 1998.

Nash, Jay Robert. *Bloodletters and Badmen*. New York: M. Evans and Co., 1973.

Silverstein, Herma. *Threads of Evidence: Using Forensic Science to Solve Crimes*. New York: Twenty-First Century Books, 1996.

Symons, Julian. *A Pictorial History of Crime*. New York: Bonanza Books, 1966.

Index

Index

Picture Credits

DANIEL E. HARMON is an editor and writer living in Spartanburg, South Carolina. He has written several books on humor and history, and has contributed historical and cultural articles to the *New York Times*, *Music Journal*, *Nautilus*, and many other periodicals. He is the managing editor of *Sandlapper: The Magazine of South Carolina* and is editor of *The Lawyer's PC* newsletter. His books include *Civil War Leaders* and *Fighting Units of the American War of Independence*.

AUSTIN SARAT is William Nelson Cromwell Professor of Jurisprudence and Political Science at Amherst College, where he also chairs the Department of Law, Jurisprudence and Social Thought. Professor Sarat is the author or editor of 23 books and numerous scholarly articles. Among his books are *Law's Violence*, *Sitting in Judgment: Sentencing the White Collar Criminal*, and *Justice and Injustice in Law and Legal Theory*. He has received many academic awards and held several prestigious fellowships. He is President of the Law & Society Association and Chair of the Working Group on Law, Culture and the Humanities. In addition, he is a nationally recognized teacher and educator whose teaching has been featured in the *New York Times*, on the *Today* show, and on National Public Radio's *Fresh Air*.